ADVANC

"I've spent the better part of a decade advising companies around the world on how to win, retain and grow customers. One question that I'm often asked is whether the best service a company can provide really *is* no service at all. Sure, it's good for our businesses to not have to engage in reactive problem-solving and fire-fighting, but how will our customers ever understand and value the service you provide if nothing ever goes wrong? In this fascinating sequel to *The Digital Wrap*, ServiceTrade's Billy Marshall lays out a powerful plan for how to get paid – and paid a premium – by your customers by maximizing your company's 'Marketing Impressions Per Service' using the latest digital technologies and channels. I'd strongly recommend this for any company in the service business looking to grow customer retention and share of wallet."

~ Matt Dixon, Chief Product & Research Officer, Tethr. Best-selling author of *The Challenger Sale* and *The Effortless Experience*

A well-crafted story makes us feel good, and the effect of customer service should be the same - a good feeling about the company. In this powerfully-argued book, Billy Marshall and Shawn Mims explain how the science of storytelling can transform the art of customer service.

~ Jonathan Gottschall, Distinguished Fellow, English Department, Washington & Jefferson College. Author of *The Storytelling Animal* and *The Professor in the Cage*

"Do we really still wait for the phone to ring and hope that a customer has an imminent HVAC catastrophe on their hands so that we can save the day? Unfortunately, the break/fix model remains the dominant source of service revenue today, but technology is beginning to change that model while simultaneously raising customer expectations for better outcomes. Brandt is committed to this change, and we read the future in the pages of both *The Digital Wrap* and *Money for Nothing*. Billy and his team have become a great partner to us in our quest for customer service leadership through technology."

~ Steve Hayes, Senior Vice President, Brandt Companies

"Firetrol Protection Systems, along with our parent company, the Minimax Viking Group, enjoy a reputation for doing things the right way, and our customers trust us with maintaining their critical fire safety equipment at their highest value facilities. Even with our market leading position, however, we discovered that we could not remain competitive in a world being influenced every day by Amazon and Uber without embracing a better online customer experience. The concepts and strategies in *The Digital Wrap* and *Money for Nothing* provide us with both the inspiration and the practical toolkit that we rely upon to sustain and enhance our market leadership."

~ Richard Felton, Regional Vice President, Firetrol Protection Systems, Inc.

MONEY FOR NOTHING

How a digital wrap earns more
pay for less work

Billy Marshall and
Shawn Mims

THOMAS NOBLE
BOOKS

Wilmington, DE

Author Contact: ServiceTrade.com

Thomas Noble Books
Wilmington, DE
www.thomasnoblebooks.com
Library of Congress Control Number: XXXXXXX
ISBN: 978-1-945586-15-6
First Printing: 2018
Editing by Gwen Hoffnagle
Cover Design by Sarah Barrie, Cyanotype.ca
Internal Design by Balaji Selvadurai

TABLE OF CONTENTS

Introduction: The Feel-Good Business Model that Delivers Money for Nothing.. 1

Chapter 1: Science Says Tell a Story to Sell a Service............................ 9

Chapter 2: Good Is Not Good Enough; "Feel Good" Is the New Customer Service Standard for Premium Brands...................... 19

Chapter 3: Avoid the Service-Call Trap; How Red Hat Created a Billion-Dollar Brand with a Money-for-Nothing Story.................. 29

Chapter 4: Shawn says, "Better Technicians and Better Service Are Not What Customers Want! How Domino's Whacked Papa John's Pizza with Better Information.".................................. 39

Chapter 5: Shawn says, "Who Do You Think You Are? If You Don't Know, Your Customers Don't Know Either.".................. 53

Chapter 6: Tellin' Ain't Sellin'; Every Customer Is from Missouri, So Show Them Something! 65

Chapter 7: How Many? How Much? How Long?; Tracking the Metrics that Measure the Value of Your Brand.............. 73

Chapter 8: Applying the Bank Bandit Test for Technology Investments 93

Chapter 9: Growing Is Better than Grinding; The Tangible and Intangible Benefits of a Growth Strategy.. 105

Chapter 10: Shawn says, "Easy to Find, Easy to Hire"; Using Your Digital Wrap to Win the Battle for Talent..................... 113

Chapter 11: AI, IoT, Big Data, and the Alphabet Soup of Technology Jargon You Need to Understand 125

Chapter 12: A Brand in the Hand Is the Future of Premium Customer Service; Getting Ready to Run a Mobile Marathon 137

Conclusion: The Significant Objects Project 149

About the Authors.. 155

THE FEEL-GOOD BUSINESS MODEL THAT DELIVERS MONEY FOR NOTHING

Dire Straits released the song *Money for Nothing* in 1985. It rocketed to the top of the US Billboard Hot 100 where it held the number-one spot for three weeks. The video for the song was a first of its kind – computer-generated animation featuring a couple of blue-collar delivery guys and a dog. *Money for Nothing* won the award for best video at the third annual MTV Video Music Awards, and it was the first song to be played for the launch of MTV in Europe. It achieved critical acclaim as well, winning the band a Grammy Award in 1986 for Best Rock Performance by Duo or Group with Vocal. No doubt you have heard the song or seen the popular video, but have you heard the story behind the song?

Mark Knopfler, the lead guitarist, vocalist, and front man for Dire Straits, was standing in an appliance store in New York City watching MTV on a wall of televisions at the back of the store. According to one report, Motley Crüe, one of the eighties' classic big hair bands, was playing on the screens. A delivery guy dressed in overalls, a ball cap, and work boots ambled over to where Mark was standing and joined him in his review of the big hair performers and their video. After a few moments watching together in silence, the delivery guy nudged Mark, pointed at the screen and declared:

> That ain't workin'. That's the way you do it. You play the guitar on the MTV. Aww, that ain't working. That's the way you do it. Money for nothing and your chicks for free.

Mark immediately began memorializing the delivery guy's poetry; he borrowed pen and paper from a store clerk and sat down at one of the kitchen displays in the store to write down everything the blue-collar poet uttered. Another appliance delivery guy joined the fray, and the two workers continued to express their admiration for the onscreen rockers, noting that they had airplanes and earned millions of dollars, all the while lamenting the meager wages paid for the backbreaking toil of delivering and installing microwave ovens and custom kitchens.

Knopfler set the blue-collar poetry to music, enlisted Sting to sing background vocals, made a groundbreaking computer-animated video for MTV, and sold over 30 million copies of the *Brothers in Arms* album that featured the song *Money for Nothing*. Isn't it ironic that Dire Straits made so much money from the poetic utterances of the blue-collar workers? The success of the song proves the wisdom of the blue-collar musings. Why do rock stars get paid so much money anyway? How is it that they always get the girl, or boy, as the case may be? Why is their business model so much more scalable and lucrative than the physical toil of blue-collar delivery workers?

The reason rockers get more pay for less work is because they have a great business model. They are not selling labor or physical products. They are selling something that makes us feel good. We like the way the rhythm and rhyme of their musical stories make us feel when we listen.

Back in the eighties when Dire Straits recorded *Money for Nothing*, the commercial model for music focused on albums and CDs. These days most music is delivered electronically, and increasingly via subscription services like Apple Music, Amazon Music, Pandora, Spotify, and others. Concerts also account for some portion of the fees earned by musicians, along with royalties on other media such as compilations, musical scores, and movie soundtracks. The delivery medium, however, is pretty irrelevant because the primary measure for how much a song earns is how many people like the experience of the song. The customer pays to play it over and over again to get that good feeling. It's not about owning the vinyl record, the shiny CD, the cassette tape, the iPod listing, or any other physical representation of the song; it's about being able to play it, on demand, whenever the mood calls for that tune.

It's not just music that makes us feel good. Similar to rock stars, movie stars also get paid lots of money for their art. Movies and television shows stir our feelings and have a powerful impact on us. There is lots of scientific research that demonstrates our attraction to the rhythm and rhyme of the rocker and the images and stories of the movie star. We don't need scientific research to know it is powerful, however, because we experience the innate power of music and stories every day. How do we teach children the alphabet? They learn by singing it. Have you noticed that it is far easier to learn the words of a song than to memorize a speech or a random selection of text? It is also far easier to recall the details of a picture image than the details of a series of bullet points in a presentation. Why? Because music, stories, and images impress us more directly than structured, written communications. Humans are born with the ability to absorb the information conveyed in rhythm, rhyme, images, and stories.

We are particularly attracted to stories that portray experiences we otherwise cannot easily achieve in our normal lives. We pay billions of dollars every year to watch movies that allow us to feel the emotion of dramatic circumstances – gunfights, airplane crashes, alien encounters, drug smuggling, espionage – while avoiding the real danger that comes with actually experiencing those high-risk situations firsthand. Almost any popular movie follows the same general formula: a hero or heroine faces a daunting or dangerous challenge and makes a big effort to overcome trouble. Think about the last five movies you watched. Did they generally hue to the formula of hero overcomes trouble to win some reward? I bet they did. Anyone who gives us an experience that stimulates our senses or helps us learn from turmoil while avoiding the genuine risks that come with real trouble can earn premium pay.

This is the lesson for the service contractor. If you want to earn premium pay for the results you deliver, give the customer a good story. Your story needs to show the customer the trouble they avoid by hiring you. The only scalable way to deliver your service story is via the internet using the information you collect – photos, videos, audios – to reinforce the smart decision the customer made when choosing your brand. You don't have to sing and dance like the rocker, but you do need to demonstrate the results your service program achieves through an online story that makes the customer feel good about your brand.

Think about it for a minute… the customer essentially wants a hassle-free experience in which nothing bad happens to the equipment that you expertly maintain for them. They really *do not* want to summon you to repair broken equipment because they would *strongly* prefer that the equipment never break down. They *do not* want to call you and relay a problem and receive assurances from a dispatcher that someone will be there shortly to begin working on the faulty equipment. They *do not* want any problems and they *do not* want to think about your company at all if they can help it.

What's the problem with perfect equipment performance and nothing bad ever happening? If nothing ever goes wrong and the customer never has to call about broken equipment, all the hard work your company does to do things the right way and assure perfect performance can be taken for granted by the customer. If they do not somehow see all the hard work that went into assuring perfect performance, they might believe nothing happened at all – no equipment failures *and* no hard work by your company. If nothing ever goes wrong, and the customer never has to think about your company, how can your company be valuable to them?

When nothing goes wrong because of your excellent preventative maintenance program, your company becomes vulnerable to the low-price guy in your market. You can almost hear the customer responding to the low-price pitch of One Truck Chuck now: "You're right, Chuck! Nothing bad ever happens around here! I am definitely paying these other guys way too much! Why shouldn't I take your low-price service offer and save a little money?"

Doing everything right and ensuring that nothing ever breaks down is not enough to save your relationship with your customer from Chuck's low-price pitch and the customer's worst instincts.

You have to give them something to stimulate their brain – just like the rocker does with a song – by presenting the story of your services through your digital wrap.

In my first book, *The Digital Wrap: Get Out of the Truck and Go Online to Own Your Customers*, I defined the concept of a digital wrap and set the context for why it should be embraced by service contractors. Everyone knows that a truck wrap is how service contractors use their vehicles to project their brand promise and contact information to customers and prospects without asking the technician to do any extra work. It's good, low-cost advertising. When the customer sees the vehicle in the parking lot, they assume some valuable service is being delivered by the contractor. The problem with a truck wrap is that it is fleeting – when the truck leaves the parking lot, the impression quickly fades. The customer soon forgets that something good might have happened. The truck wrap also does not provide any insight into what valuable service might have been provided that day. The truck wrap does not tell a story.

A digital wrap, by contrast, is memorable and specific. Your technicians are already creating electronic records of their work to send back to the office via email, text, spreadsheet, photo, video, etc. using their smartphones. If you use this material online to share the story of your work with your customers, you have a digital wrap. Because it is online, the digital wrap is easy to search, review, recall, engage, forward, and use to impress the customer with the value of your service program. It can be created with no extra work from your technicians and office staff, making it easy on your team. A digital wrap is permanent and sticky because of the power of the Internet, which is a huge advantage compared to the truck wrap.

The digital wrap does something else as well – something very important. It shows the customer the trouble they avoided because your company is on the job. This presentation of trouble that was caught before it became a real problem stimulates the customer's human craving for drama and action without actually exposing them to the disruption that comes with real drama and action – broken pipes, system dumps, seized motors, frozen coils, etc. The customer feels good about your brand because your digital wrap provides a memorable story to review and share. Everyone loves a good story, preferably one with lots of drama in which the hero (your technician) overcomes perilous challenges (deficient equipment) to save the day. Stories make us feel good, and the good feelings engendered through your digital wrap allow your company to charge a premium for the labor and parts you are providing with your service program. The extra amount you can charge for a feel-good story is "money for nothing" – just like the rocker's business model.

In *Money for Nothing*, Shawn Mims, ServiceTrade's director of marketing and its longest-serving employee, and me, Billy Marshall, tell you a series of stories that demonstrate why the concepts behind a digital wrap are so effective in increasing the value of a service contracting brand. We present lessons from mega brands like Facebook, Domino's, Red Hat, Amazon, BMW, and others that can be applied to your commercial service contracting business to make it more scalable and more valuable. We show you how the science behind the human attraction to music and story can be applied to deliver a more satisfying and valuable experience to your customers.

Money for Nothing gives you simple ideas and formulas to move your value proposition beyond vague sales promises and invoices crammed with mind-numbing details regarding labor and materials. We help you define and build the value of your brand so you can charge a premium price and attract new customers – all with zero additional effort from your technicians and your administrative staff. "Money for Nothing" is not just a chart-topping, critically acclaimed rock-and-roll song. It is also a catchy slogan for how a digital wrap will earn your business more pay for less work.

CHAPTER 1

SCIENCE SAYS TELL A STORY TO SELL A SERVICE

Purposeful storytelling isn't show business, it's good business.
— *Peter Guber, CEO of Mandalay Entertainment*

If rock stars get paid like rock stars because their music makes us feel good, what should a service contractor do to make the customer feel good – and get paid like a rock star? The best way to answer that question is to understand why music makes us feel good, and then do something similar, because no one really expects you to sing and dance. That would be weird. So why does music make us feel good? Why does a song pump us up? Or break us down? Why are we moved by music?

In his excellent book, *This Is Your Brain on Music*, Daniel Levitin argues that music moves us because our genes are programmed to respond to it based on hundreds of thousands of years of evolution. Music apparently existed before structured language. In the days of the cavemen, music was a way for guys to woo girls at the community fire or in front of the entrance to the cave dwelling. Funny how little has changed over hundreds of thousands of years.

Musical creativity is apparently a predictor of health and wealth, both of which can be useful in surviving the challenges of life. We are drawn to rock stars and other talented musicians and artists because we perceive them to be good mates. We want to have sex with them and have children with them. Seriously. It is human nature. How else can you explain the hordes of attractive women who are seduced by an ugly, scrawny guy like Mick Jagger? How is it that Julia Roberts was somehow attracted enough to Lyle Lovett to marry him? Fortunately there is a scientific explanation for these cases of beautiful women being drawn to these creative but very ugly guys. In his book, Levitin references a clever experiment conducted by cognitive psychologists Geoffrey Miller of the University of New Mexico and Martie Haselton of UCLA. Their experiment essentially amounted to a game of "who would you rather" in which they described two men to a group of women and then asked the women, "Who would you rather have sex with?"

Levitin explains that there were two intriguing aspects of the game. First, the potential male sex partners were only presented as written descriptions – there were no pictures to influence attractiveness. One man was described as a very creative and skilled artist, but due to bad luck he was financially poor. The other man was merely average on the creative talent scale, but due to good luck he was financially wealthy. It was made clear to the women that his wealth was not the result of some skill or capability. So who did the women choose? Well, what I haven't told you yet is the other intriguing aspect of the experiment: Miller and Haselton also asked the women where they were in their monthly ovulation cycle. The fertile women demonstrated a clear preference for the poor, talented artist. The other women demonstrated no preference between the two men. (https://www.researchgate.net/publication/225821618_ Women%27s_Fertility_across_the_Life_Cycle_Increases_the_ Short-Term_Attractiveness_of_Creative_Intelligence)

Somehow it is always about sex, right? There's a reason for that. Two essential characteristics determine who we have evolved to be as a human species. First, you cannot pass your genes along unless you have sex with someone who is capable of producing offspring, assuming you yourself are fertile. Second, those offspring have to likewise survive and then have offspring who also survive and produce offspring, and so on and so forth. We are programmed to seek sex partners who will yield offspring who survive to become effective sex partners who produce and then nurture their offspring. For some reason – and Levitin explores many of the possibilities in his book – musical creativity is an indicator of a good mate. Music moves us because we are hardwired through evolution to be emotionally stirred by it. Levitin covers a lot of ground in his book, and I think it is great reading for anyone who wants to understand why our love for music is fundamental to human nature. The simple lesson for *Money for Nothing* purposes, however, is that we love music because it lights up our brains in a pleasurable way that is deep-seated and innate to who we are as humans. Music just makes us feel good.

If you want to get paid like a rock star, light up the customer's brain in a pleasurable way. You need to make them feel good. If you are not going to sing and dance, what can you do to create the same feel-good brain state as the rocker's music? How can you associate your service brand with pleasurable feelings? Fortunately there is a simple answer. Music is not the only medium that lights up our brains. Humans are also programmed to be moved by stories and images.

The same cavemen who were dancing and singing to woo the cavegirls, or vice versa, were also telling stories and making cave drawings and sculptures. It turns out that hearing or seeing a good story lights up the same pleasurable areas of the brain as actually experiencing the events of the story. We literally "feel" what we see and hear. This phenomenon is associated with something called mirror neurons, which were discovered accidentally when scientists noticed that monkey brains experienced the same stimulation when the monkeys were reaching for a banana that they did when the monkeys watched another monkey or a person reach for a banana. Our brains literally love the mental exercise provided by good stories. Seeing and hearing a good story is almost as pleasurable as living the experience reflected by the story.

If a story lights up our brains in the same manner as actually experiencing the story, more books and movies would simply be about hot sex and good food, right? No doubt there is a market for pornography (if images and stories didn't light up our brains similarly to the actual experience, pornography wouldn't be popular, would it?), but in most cases the stories that attract us are about adversity and dramatic circumstances. Have you noticed that most movies and popular books of fiction deal with challenging and troublesome situations? Perhaps there is an evolutionary component in our attraction to stories that is similar to our attraction to music. Maybe stories that depict trouble help us survive a world full of trouble, and likewise help our offspring survive.

In his book *The Storytelling Animal: How Stories Make Us Human*, Jonathan Gottschall explores why stories, like music, are so important to humans. Storytelling – like the preference for a creative, artistic mate – is an evolutionary mechanism to help humans learn and mentally practice survival skills that enable us to mate and nurture our offspring, so they can survive to ultimately mate and nurture their offspring, and so on and so forth. Practicing survival activities through stories lights up our brains just like the pleasurable experience of music does. Gottschall describes how children, from an early age, create stories as part of their play activities. It's interesting that children's playtime stories and playacting are almost always nightmarish in content.

Have you ever considered how gruesome many of the original children's fairy tales are? The story of *Hansel and Gretel* describes a witch fattening up the kids on candy to make a meal of them. Or *Little Red Riding Hood*, in which a wolf eats Granny and later gets killed by a lumberjack. Or *Jack and the Beanstalk*, in which a giant can sniff out humans for the purpose of grinding their bones to make bread. Kids love these gruesome tales that are full of troublesome violence. From the earliest age we practice storytelling and playacting in the context of troublesome situations. We are born to enjoy trouble.

It makes sense if you think about the most popular movies, television shows, and books. They are almost universally about some troublesome situation. Gottschall summarizes it nicely in his book:

> Stories the world over are almost always about people ... with problems. The people want something badly – to survive, to win the girl or boy, to find a lost child. But big obstacles loom between the protagonists and what they want. Just about any story – comic, tragic, romantic – is about a protagonist's efforts to secure, usually at some cost, what he or she desires.

We spend billions of dollars on books and movies that take our mind on a journey into a troubling situation and depict the efforts of a hero to cast the trouble aside and secure a hard-fought reward. We are hopelessly attracted to the mental distraction of a good story or a good song. So if you want to get paid like a rock star or a movie star, give your customer a story that lights up their brain and makes them feel good.

How are you going to do that? The answer is certainly not by enrolling all your technicians and office staff in a creative writing course. They won't write anything down anyway, and if they did the customer probably wouldn't read it. Remember, the power of story was programmed into us long before there was anything resembling written communication. The printing press was not invented until the fifteenth century, so storytelling existed long before stories were widely distributed as text in books. The answer to this how-to-tell-a-story riddle is right in front of your nose, or at least in front of the nose of the teenager closest to you right now.

My three teenaged daughters wreck my Verizon data plan each month. I feel totally helpless to curb their consumption, and they will pay almost any price to avoid reducing their data usage. I literally charge them fees for their overages, and they happily pay instead of changing their behavior. What are they consuming? It isn't text; it's music and – wait for it – pictures and videos. Pictures and videos tell the stories they want to see and hear. My daughters also use pictures and videos to create stories to share with their friends (hence the fees I pay for storage, which are thankfully much cheaper than bandwidth fees). Facebook has become the fifth most valuable company in the world on the foundation of letting us easily create and share stories online through pictures and videos. Hidden among all those Facebook stories is clickbait attracting you and me to some product for sale by someone disguising the product among a series of related stories.

We cannot deny our human nature. We are drawn to music, rhythm, rhyme, stories, and images because of deep-seated human tendencies. Embrace the inevitable pull of your brand into the realm of online storytelling based on this scientific explanation for why humans behave as they do. It works for Facebook, it works for Amazon (try to find something for sale on Amazon without pictures and reviews), and it will work for your brand, too. It's how you are going to engage customers with your troublesome findings about their critical equipment, and how you will entice them with clickbait that demonstrates that you can take care of everything so long as they keep paying the price of your excellent maintenance program.

Consider for a moment what a customer currently gets when they buy into your service program. If you are doing what most contractors do, and you are doing it well, the customer receives two things: 1) nothing, and 2) invoices. Nothing is the perfect outcome: nothing ever breaks, and all their equipment performs flawlessly – no breakdowns, no emergencies, no hassles, and no disruptions in their business. Maybe they see your truck with your logo in the parking lot every once in a while. Maybe the technician checks in before beginning an inspection or routine maintenance. Chances are, however, they do not actually witness anything valuable that you deliver. They are getting nothing from you. They do, however, get your invoices in their email (or, God forbid, via snail mail – ugh!). Invoices generally present cryptic descriptions of your accounting codes and the amount owed to you for the "nothing" you delivered.

Do you imagine their brain lighting up with pleasurable good feelings about your brand based on what they get when they buy into your service program? A truck in the parking lot? Emails with invoices attached? No positive brain stimulation anywhere in sight? This business model does not come close to the feel-good of the rock star or the storytelling/selling of Facebook. Selling invoices for nothing sucks. Let me repeat that for effect – *selling invoices for nothing sucks.*

To get money for nothing, science says that you have to tell a story to sell a service. The more troublesome the content of your stories, the more you will light up the customer's brain, and the more they will reward your brand for the great experience. Don't just deliver the nothing that represents the best outcome; give the customer plenty of drama to demonstrate the hard-fought battle you waged to achieve their reward of perfect equipment performance with no hassles or aggravation.

Every skilled technician I have ever met can usually describe dozens of ways to improve the configuration or condition of any particular system. So let them do that for the customer. Each engagement with the customer's equipment should yield photos and audios and videos that tell a story about how your service activities saved the day. Dirty filters are now clean. Low pressure (evidenced by a photo of the gauge) is now up to the manufacturer's specifications. Excessive grease buildup is now clean. High temperature is now in normal operating range. High amperage is now normal amperage (evidenced by a photo of the meter). Don't just do the work; *tell the story* to sell the service. Light up their brain with the mental stimulation of the real trouble you put down. Take them up onto the roof, into the ductwork, inside the riser room, into the control panel, inside the chiller unit... without them ever leaving the comfortable perch where they happen to be sitting when they review your online story.

The key element of an effective digital wrap is that all these stories have to be collected and delivered to the customer with minimal extra administrative burden. If you haven't already invested in systems that make it easy to record and deliver the story online, this approach will not work for your brand. Your technicians and office administrators will not do extra work to deliver the story and your customer will not take extra steps to review the story. When my teenaged girls use Instagram or Snapchat, their audience systematically gets the content without having to burrow around online for it. Your customers should benefit similarly. And just like these platforms, interspersed with these stories will be subtle (or not-so-subtle in some cases) offers for them to buy more service so their equipment continues to perform flawlessly, such as online repair quotes that show troublesome signs of equipment decay through photos and videos.

It is human nature to be moved by music and enthralled by stories. Customers don't expect you to sing and dance, but your brand will become more valuable to them when your service engages their brains with good stories about the trouble you put down through your valuable maintenance routine. How are you going to do that? We have some ideas for you.

Now that we have explained the science behind the feel-good sales approach of the rockers and the movie stars, the balance of *Money for Nothing* reviews interesting case studies of companies that created scalable businesses selling "nothing" coupled with a premium brand experience that makes the customer feel good. We also provide basic advice and principles about how to build and sell a premium program that matches the brand promise you are passionate about delivering. Finally we show you how to easily measure your progress as you initiate programs to earn more pay for less work. Best of all, most of the work you do to build the value of your company with a money-for-nothing digital wrap strategy is fun, especially when you begin to get feedback from customers that your unique brand of service is lighting up their brains in ways that make your company indispensable to them.

CHAPTER 2

GOOD IS NOT GOOD ENOUGH; "FEEL GOOD" IS THE NEW CUSTOMER SERVICE STANDARD FOR PREMIUM BRANDS

I've learned that people will forget what you said, people will forget what you did, but people will never forget how you made them feel.
— Maya Angelou

Jeff Bezos, the founder of Amazon, is the wealthiest person on the planet. He owns about 17 percent of Amazon, and that stake is worth about $115 billion. Amazon was founded in 1994, so Jeff has amassed this fortune in just 24 years. Wow! I bring up the example of Jeff Bezos as a wealth-building machine because his views on customer service have turned Amazon into one of the most powerful brands of our generation, and other premium brands are lining up behind Amazon in an escalating battle for customer service supremacy.

Great customer service is not a fad at Amazon; Jeff Bezos has been talking about it for a long time. Here are a handful of his quotes on the subject:

> If there's one reason we have done better than our peers in the Internet space over the last six years, it is because we have focused like a laser on customer experience.

> We see our customers as invited guests to a party, and we are the hosts. It's our job every day to make every important aspect of the customer experience a little bit better.

> The best customer service is if the customer doesn't need to call you, doesn't need to talk to you. It just works.

> We've had three big ideas at Amazon that we've stuck with for eighteen years, and they're the reason we're successful: Put the customer first. Invent. And be patient.

Many of these are old quotes dating back to as early as 2000. Amazon does not settle for "good" in the realm of customer service. It is not enough for the customer to simply get what they paid to receive. Amazon wants customers to enjoy the experience in the same manner as a guest might enjoy a good party. Great brands now want to copy Amazon because Jeff Bezos has become the wealthiest guy in the world due to the crazy success of Amazon stock. Smart business owners want the same value for their shareholders, so they are behaving like Amazon and aiming well beyond the idea of simply satisfying the customer. They truly want their customers to *feel good* about the experience of buying from them. This current obsession with the customer experience is certainly a good thing for customers. Because so many companies are now focusing on innovation in customer service, the bar for feel-good status is climbing higher every day.

The most popular approach today for measuring customer satisfaction is the Net Promoter Score, or NPS. Wikipedia reports that more than two-thirds of the Fortune 1000 is currently using NPS. Here's how it works:

Customers are asked a single, simple question: How likely is it that you would recommend our company/product/service to a friend or colleague? They are given a rating scale from 0 to 10 to answer the question. Zero means the customer would never recommend the company to a friend or colleague, and 10 means they would absolutely recommend the company to a friend or colleague.

Respondents are then categorized into the following groups:

- Promoters: those who score the business with a 9 or 10 (likely to promote to others)
- Passives: with scores of 7 or 8 (not likely to benefit or harm your brand)
- Detractors: with scores of 6 or less (liabilities for your brand)

The final NPS is calculated by subtracting the percentage of Detractors from the percentage of Promoters, with the Passives not contributing at all to the score. As an example, if you were to survey 100 customers and 35 score as Detractors (0 to 6), 25 score as Passives (7 or 8), and 40 score as Promoters (9 or 10), your NPS would be:

Promoters - Detractors = NPS   40 - 35 = 5

Your NPS for this survey sample is a 5. Anything above 0 is considered to be positive, and a score approaching 50 is terrific.

The NPS is probably a little too simplistic, and you can find lots of criticism of the science of NPS from survey theory experts if you look for it online. My opinion and those of the critics are not what really matters in this case. What is important is that two-thirds of the Fortune 1000 are relying on this information in one form or another to help them improve customer satisfaction. Lots of big brands with big budgets are focusing lots of energy on measuring customer satisfaction. The other important thing to note is that this wildly popular tool skews heavily toward "feel good" as the goal for customer service. Only scores of 9 and 10 are credited positively, and anything less than a 7 is negative. I think anyone who scores a company with a 9 or a 10 feels really good about their experience. So two-thirds of Fortune 1000 companies is scheming for ways to get more scores of 9 and 10 because that is the only way to improve their NPS. That's a lot of companies with a lot of focus on making customers feel good about their brand.

What does this emphasis on outstanding customer service mean for you? Your customer service efforts are going to be compared to those of Amazon and two-thirds of the Fortune 1000 because they are all "focused like a laser" on customer experience these days. NPS is hot because customer service innovations are hot because customer loyalty is hot because growth is hot because Amazon is hot. Customers are not going to compare you to your always-go-low-on-price competitor down the street any longer. They are going to ask, "Why can't you be more like Amazon and give me notifications when I am due for service or when the technician is en route to my location?" The customer service bar is being set by the sum of all of the best experiences the customer has ever encountered across all companies in both their personal and professional life.

The good news is that most customer service innovations can be observed and imitated if they fit your idea of great customer service. The case of Amazon is particularly intriguing because up until a few years ago Amazon had absolutely no influence over the products customers were buying from them. They were simply a reseller of other companies' products. Any innovation they delivered to make a customer feel good was not a product innovation but one focused on improving the buying experience. Here are a few feel-good customer service themes direct from Amazon that should be among the guideposts you use in establishing your feel-good customer service strategy:

Pictures and videos: Amazon understands the psychology of human decision-making as detailed in the last chapter. Images impress us. They help us understand our environment and make decisions. We are more easily impressed by images and stories than we are by bullet points and descriptive prose. I challenge you to find anything for sale on Amazon that does not include at least one picture. Generally there are several, and Amazon gives you tools to zoom and pan to get a better view of the details that might interest you. It is easier to feel good about a purchase when you can see the images that reinforce your buying decision. Increasingly video is also becoming a part of the purchase review because it combines imagery with a story about the product.

Reviews: Reviews are the stories other customers share about their experience with the product. Like images, stories are a powerful learning mechanism for humans. By reading the stories, we get comfortable with the experience we can expect from the product. We also understand any trouble we might face through these review stories. Reviews further empower customers because a poor customer service experience and a bad review is often the catalyst for a company to correct the problem. Holding the company accountable for a good experience through a review process gives customers more comfort at the time of purchase.

Convenience: One of Amazon's first innovations was one-click purchasing. They applied for and were awarded a method patent on this invention back in 1999. Amazon famously sued Barnes and Noble when they copied the innovation. Amazon had streamlined the purchase process by eliminating the hassle of checkout, and the company was not going to stand by quietly when their fiercest competitor copied this innovation. Now the company offers a mobile app (of course) so customers can easily browse and buy from their phones. Amazon also provides multiple delivery and gift options; smart speakers that do many things in addition to letting you buy using Alexa commands; push-button buying using a little connected clicker called a Dash Button to order items routinely purchased, like laundry detergent; and many more buying innovations. The company is even experimenting with delivery by drone. Eliminating all the barriers between your customer's money and your bank account just makes sense.

No-hassle returns: Amazon never argues with a customer regarding a request to return an item as long as there is some reason for the rejection (fit, color, quality, whatever). They make returns easy with a self-service process on their website. Customers feel better about placing an order when they know they can return the product if something is not right.

Mobile experience: Amazon enhances convenience with their mobile app because shopping is always available. Most customers are never more than three feet from their phone, and therefore I believe the mobile option is worthy of its own feel-good category. Because my smartphone has a camera and a microphone, I can take photos, scan barcodes, and use verbal commands to search for products. I can manage every aspect of my relationship with Amazon through my mobile device, which means I can manage it anywhere and anytime.

Feel good by doing good: The AmazonSmile program allows me to select a charity to receive a donation from Amazon equal to .5 percent of my qualifying purchases when I begin my shopping at smile.amazon.com. Do you imagine that a customer feels good when they begin their shopping experience by typing "smile" and then direct a contribution to a favorite charity when they buy something? It's easy to feel good when your vendor helps you do good.

Notifications and visibility: Amazon gives customers a number of ways to track their orders and their order history. Any shopping activity, whether resulting in a purchase or not, generally results in some level of follow-up from Amazon. When I place an order, Amazon continuously informs me of the status, beginning with a "thank you" order confirmation. They send a shipment notice plus an arrival notice. If I shop and do not order, Amazon often follows up with deals on items I viewed, hoping to push me over the edge to buy the product. After I receive a purchase, I am generally offered an opportunity to review the purchase, and typically offered several complementary items. (Shawn goes into more detail about these *marketing impressions per service* (MIPS) in chapter 4.) Beyond the notifications, Amazon tracks my purchases so I can reference that information to make decisions regarding future purchases. All of this attention and account visibility certainly helps the customer feel good about their relationship with Amazon.

Subscription membership: Amazon offers customers a subscription program called Prime. Prime bundles all manner of Amazon services and benefits into a subscription program for which customers pay an annual membership fee. The subscription offers access to a library of books and music along with lower costs (usually free) for shipping and guaranteed two-day delivery for any purchases. Statista, the online statistics portal, estimates that Amazon had 95 million US Prime members as of June 2018. That amounts to nearly 70 percent of US households participating in Prime. Chapter 5 covers Prime in more detail, but the key takeaway for our feel-good story is that it feels good to be a member of a club with a wide range of benefits. Another key takeaway is that a subscription business model with its predictable and guaranteed cash flow is a powerful foundation on which to build a dominant brand.

Several dozen books (at least) have been written about the Amazon phenomenon, and I could probably go on and on myself about the lessons that can be drawn from its success. The lesson for the service contractor is that making your customers feel good about your service will likely lead to greater riches for you and your company. Jeff Bezos is the richest guy in the world, and he has been pretty clear that his success comes from innovations that make the customer feel good about doing business with Amazon. Many of these innovations are directly applicable to your business, and you should take inspiration from them to deliver your own version of feel-good customer service.

In the next chapter we look at another giant brand that delivered a unique innovation to the market and created a multibillion-dollar company in the process. Red Hat is probably one of the best examples of how to charge a premium price for a service program in which the best outcome for both customer and supplier is that nothing ever happens. When nothing happens it means that everything just works as expected. When you combine the feel-good customer service lessons from Amazon with the "nothing bad ever happens" of Red Hat, you have a strong foundation for a valuable service brand.

CHAPTER 3

AVOID THE SERVICE-CALL TRAP; HOW RED HAT CREATED A BILLION-DOLLAR BRAND WITH A MONEY-FOR-NOTHING STORY

The bigger the problem, the bigger the reward.
You should dream big because that's where the big rewards are.
— Bob Young, co-founder of Red Hat

I left IBM to join Red Hat in late November of 1998. Red Hat would record $5 million in revenue in 1998 selling a software collection on compact discs (CDs) to computer science enthusiasts in retail outlets like Frye's, CompUSA, Egghead, and Best Buy. All the software on the CDs was also available free online, but in those days the Internet was still slow for most people, and installing the software from purchased CDs was faster and easier. The collection included helpful user manuals to assist with installation and setup (actual paper booklets back in those days). Fast-forward 20 years to today, and almost all the software Red Hat sells is still available for free on the Internet, and the Internet is lightning fast, which eliminates the download hassle. But somehow Red Hat is a worldwide enterprise worth more than $20 billion with annual sales of about $3 billion. How can Red Hat make so much money for something that is available for free? Because Red Hat is a money-for-nothing premium brand. Let's have a look at how they do it.

One of my first tasks after I joined Red Hat was to determine why all those computer geeks liked Red Hat so much, and what, if anything, the company might sell to them or their employers that was worth more than the $50 they were spending on a CD collection at the store. Shelley Bainter, who works with me here at ServiceTrade, alongside Hilary Stokes and Marty Wesley, began setting up "customer Friday" events every week to quiz Red Hat customers and users about their experiences with the technology and the company. Our goal was to understand what was important to them and determine how Red Hat might use that information to make a more valuable product. We were in a bit of a hurry to figure it out because the company had an initial public offering of stock on the NASDAQ exchange in August of 1999, and the shares jumped from about $20 per share to about $150 per share in a few short weeks. With huge expectations and a monster market capitalization of about $20 billion, it was critical that my group deliver on a premium product strategy. We still had no clue what to sell to potential customers, and we certainly did not want the shareholders to figure out that we didn't know what we were doing.

Well, we didn't figure it out fast enough. The share price plummeted from $150 to about $3 over the course of the next few months. But in the midst of incredible employee anxiety and shareholder lawsuits, we discovered something from our research that proved to be very, very valuable: The more experience a customer had with Linux (the software collection that Red Hat distributed), the more they valued easy and quick access to the maintenance downloads provided by Red Hat. These highly experienced Linux users were keen to keep their server systems in top working condition. They did not want their critical servers to be susceptible to security flaws or operating errors that might disrupt their businesses. They readily indicated that they were willing to pay Red Hat a premium to be certain that nothing bad ever happened to their systems.

With validated survey information about why Red Hat was valuable to its most knowledgeable and experienced customers, my product marketing team set about defining a premium program that would allow customers to pay for a subscription to the maintenance program delivered by Red Hat engineering. While we were trying to formulate a scalable product plan, the press became involved in describing Red Hat's business model. (We couldn't yet describe it, so the press was going to fill the gap.) Red Hat was a high-flying stock before the crash, and journalist and technology pundits were keen to weigh in with their opinions about whether or not any business model would actually emerge to sustain shareholder value.

The press told the world that Red Hat sold "support" for free software. Unfortunately our customer prospects took this to mean that if their free Linux software "broke" they could call Red Hat to "fix" it. This model is known as a "break/fix" business model, and it sucks. Red Hat did not want to be in the break/fix business. Our most valuable users told us that *avoiding* system failures was most important, not fixing problems after they happened! But the break/

fix story was a simple message that was widely promoted in the technology press.

A break/fix business model is a miserable model. Customers call your company when they are under extreme duress. Every revenue opportunity for your company is an emergency that stresses out your staff as they hustle about trying to please the customer. Under this business model the entire customer relationship is stressful and challenging. The only good thing about a break/fix model is that it is easy for salespeople to talk about it, so that's what our salespeople tried to sell.

Does anything about the way the press began to describe Red Hat's business model sound like the challenges you face in your business? Your competitor – or worse, your own salespeople – tells the customer, "We will be there 24/7 when things go wrong! Just call us when you are freaking out over a disruptive equipment failure, and we will drop everything to make it good again for you!"

Don't fall into this break/fix trap. It might be easy to sell, but it's going to hurt.

Independent of the musings of the popular press regarding Red Hat's break/fix business model, my product marketing team knew what Red Hat needed to deliver to customers to become a valuable brand. We released two products in 2001 that, taken together, represented a premium subscription program. Red Hat Network was a management console that helped customers update and patch their own systems, and Red Hat Enterprise Linux was a well-defined set of free software packages for which Red Hat promised to deliver prompt and quality maintenance. We priced these based on the number of computer systems under maintenance and the type of workload these systems supported for the customer. Critical systems that could not tolerate downtime were priced higher than other systems that were simply running batch programs and could tolerate some downtime. This pricing scheme aligned the value of the system and its consistent operating performance with the price of the subscription. Perfect alignment, right? Not exactly, because the press had poisoned the market with their break/fix news story, which resulted in a lot of uncomfortable conversations with large potential customers.

The sales team was not yet comfortable swapping its break/fix conversation with all of this new messaging around maintenance and subscriptions, so I nominated myself to show them how it was done. I got my first opportunity when Cisco Systems of San Jose, California, reached out to Red Hat for suggestions about how they might simplify and streamline their Linux technology systems and applications.

The biggest deal the sales team had closed to that point was in the low six figures. When Cisco signed a multiyear seven-figure deal, the subscription formula I had used to sell it became extremely interesting to the rest of the company, especially the sales team. I happily accepted my promotion to run sales, and off I went to have a bunch of uncomfortable conversations with high-profile customer prospects.

One of the first calls I fielded was from someone who worked directly for the chief information officer for BankOne in Ohio. BankOne was one of the ten largest banks in the country, and later would merge with JPMorgan Chase to become the second biggest bank behind Citigroup. Clearly this was an important prospect for Red Hat, and they had approached us about helping them with their Linux strategy. The person responsible for Linux made it very clear to me that they were not interested in our subscription strategy but would happily sign an agreement to call us when things "broke" and they needed technical support to "fix" the problem. He wanted me to come to Ohio for a meeting. I told him there was no point in my going to Ohio because we did not offer what he was looking for. I referred him to our competition and told him to call me back if he ever had a change of heart. The CEO of Red Hat nearly lost his mind when I told him that I had refused to even take a meeting with BankOne to discuss their break/fix request. He was beginning to wonder if promoting me to run sales had been such a great idea, because BankOne was gone.

Fortunately for both me and Red Hat, I was having other conversations that were going quite well. One of them was with Rich Breunich, then the global head of technology for Citigroup, the largest financial institution in the world at the time. In a meeting with Rich and his team, I explained our maintenance business model:

> A break/fix model means we are incentivized to provide customers with technology that breaks all the time in order for us to grow our revenue. This model delivers the highest revenue when things break. But we don't want to collaborate on technology with you only when things are broken. We want to have a more thoughtful relationship in which we collaborate continuously to give you great technology that never breaks and always exceeds your expectations.

Rich's staff was having none of it. They puked on my grand vision and pounded the table. They explained to me that every major technology publication asserted in article after article that Red Hat sold support for Linux, and by God that is what they intended to buy from us. If I could not abandon my high-minded,

MIT-inspired ideas for how to fleece them with a slick Red Hat business model, they would take their millions of dollars in IT spending elsewhere.

Fortunately for me and my career, Rich was in my corner, and he settled the matter quickly by agreeing with me about the business model and their ultimate requirements for maintenance and predictability. Citigroup did not want to incentivize their vendors to deliver shoddy products in order to increase revenue from break/fix support, he explained to his staff. They would happily pay a premium for great technology that performed without aggravation. Certainly Red Hat was available when things went wrong, but that should not be the basis of the relationship. It should be the exception, not the rule.

Like Cisco, Citigroup signed a multiyear, seven-figure deal with Red Hat. Now my sales team was off to the races. They had a premium formula, premium customers in Citigroup and Cisco, and they had a leader who would back them up as they engaged in uncomfortable conversations with high-profile prospects, even if that meant walking away when a large prospect like BankOne did not agree.

Does any of the Red Hat story feel familiar? Do you find yourself selling service features that are defined by your customers and by low-end competition? Break/fix? Price? Labor rate? Parts? Do salespeople race to the lowest common denominator to declare a win – and then dump it in the lap of the service department and move on? All of these things were true for Red Hat, and yet it managed to bust out of the mold of break/fix misery and create a multibillion-dollar brand by collecting "money for nothing."

When Red Hat turned the corner financially with a scalable model, I was often dispatched to investor and press meetings to explain how we were making so much money selling free software. My message was simple: Red Hat offered customers "a predictable outcome for a predictable price." Sure, they could download a bunch of free technology from the Internet and cobble it together, and in some cases that might work out okay. In the most important cases, however, not having a reliable vendor for critical systems was not acceptable. Putting the hardware vendor in charge was also generally a bad idea, because all a hardware vendor wants to do is sell more hardware, not optimize outcomes. Hardware vendors get paid more when systems have marginal performance and the customer requires more hardware to support the load. Red Hat was perfectly positioned to help customers get the most from their hardware and systems through a technology-maintenance subscription program.

There are several important lessons in the Red Hat money-for-nothing story for the commercial service contractor:

- Break/fix support is a terrible business model. Your brand becomes associated with stress and chaos at the customer. Earning more revenue means the customer is experiencing more trouble. This model does not end well for the vendor.

- Selling what the market is buying is often not a good idea. All of Red Hat's competitors simply said yes to customers' requests for break/fix support because that was easy. They got exactly what they deserved. Almost all of them went out of business after the Linux frenzy subsided. Be willing to have the hard conversation with the customer to get a better outcome for both you and them.

- Know who you are and the value of your service model. It is not enough to say no to something that is obviously imprudent; you have to offer the customer an alternative plan. Sell them a premium program. (Chapter 5 goes into the specifics of creating, naming, marketing, and selling a premium, branded maintenance program.)

- Say no to customers who don't buy into your vision. Better still, offer them the contact information for your competitor. Let the competition sully their brand with miserable customer experiences while you strengthen yours with long-lasting and scalable relationships.

- A subscription model for a technology maintenance program is an extremely lucrative business model. Red Hat found a position of authority relative to the system vendors (Dell, HP, IBM, etc.) by offering branded, third-party system maintenance. Customers could turn to Red Hat for advice about which technology subsystems were most scalable and reliable. Service contracting is not very different from Red Hat's business. As the manufacturers in your segment seek to exert more control over customer maintenance, you need a strategy to push back and become the expert the customer trusts to deliver optimum system performance.

- Don't let the manufacturers of the hardware take your seat at the table with the customer. System vendors are generally terrible at customer service, and they are incentivized to sell more systems. Be certain you build skills and collect data across a broad swath of hardware brands so you can offer the customer the insights and outcomes they are seeking.

- Focus on engineering and innovation. The only way you will get to set the agenda (as opposed to a hardware vendor or another contractor) with the customer is if you have the expertise to optimize their outcomes through your premium service program. It is better to get paid for what you know than to get paid for where you go.

Red Hat is a terrific example of how a money-for-nothing strategy can be used to deliver incredible customer loyalty and superior business results. A subscription program gives the customer the "nothing" they want – no breakdowns, no budget surprises, optimal performance – while providing your business with a predictable, high-margin revenue stream. To achieve this outcome, however, you must we willing to reset the conversation with the customer and walk away from break/fix business that does not include a premium maintenance contract.

In the next chapter we review the Domino's case and discover how they used information, convenience, and transparency to dominate their competition. We also give you some practical ideas for the information you can share with customers as part of your digital wrap to pull them into the story of the services you're delivering. If you're going to sell a subscription program in which nothing ever happens, you need to be able to show the customer the hard work you do to keep their critical equipment in perfect condition.

CHAPTER 4

SHAWN SAYS, "BETTER TECHNICIANS AND BETTER SERVICE ARE NOT WHAT CUSTOMERS WANT! HOW DOMINO'S WHACKED PAPA JOHN'S PIZZA WITH BETTER INFORMATION."

If you don't have a competitive advantage, don't compete.
—Jack Welch, former CEO of General Electric

W ho has better pizza – Domino's or Papa John's? I do a lot of presentations about these companies, and when I pose this question to audiences, they're usually split right down the middle. Personally I'm a Domino's fan. From a value perspective, however, our individual opinions about who has better pies don't really matter. Here's what really matters:

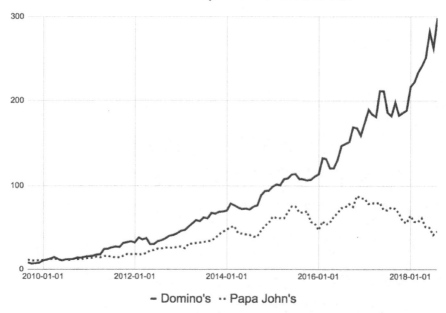

Figure 1: Domino's dominates Papa John's in stock price appreciation

Domino's is CRUSHING Papa John's, and they have been since 2009. In fact, Domino's stock has outperformed Amazon, Apple, and Google in the last nine years. For every dollar you invested in Domino's in 2009, you'd have $30 as of the writing of this book. Compare that to $10.00, $5.50, and $2.75 for Amazon, Apple, and Google respectively. Papa John's, on the other hand, would be worth a respectable $3.75, but it's been on a steady decline for the past two years.

These numbers are surprising considering the ubiquity of Papa John's marketing. It's practically impossible to watch sports without hearing their slogan: "Better ingredients, better pizza, Papa John's!" They're everywhere. Domino's spends plenty of money on advertising too, but their marketing strategy went a very different direction starting in 2009. It's best summed up by their CEO, Patrick Doyle, who has often said:

"We are as much a tech company as we are a pizza company."

What technology do you think he's talking about? Their accounting platform? Their point-of-sales systems? Their pizza ovens? No. He's talking about their customer-facing technology like their Pizza Tracker and mobile apps. While Papa John's has been pouring money into billboards, radio ads, and television advertising, Domino's hired the best web and mobile developers, built an incredible R&D team, and took a massive risk on the future of smartphones. In fact, an interview with Doyle in 2015 revealed that about 300 of their 700 employees at their corporate headquarters were focused on technology, not pizza (or accounting). Here's another one of Doyle's quotes:

"We believe by transaction counts we're in the top five of e-commerce companies in the world."

That's unbelievable for a pizza company. On the other hand, Papa John's sales are sinking and their stock price is sliding. They're trying to blame their poor financial performance on the recent drama in the NFL and the subsequent viewership decline. And it doesn't help when the CEO gets canned over inappropriate behavior either. In any case, Domino's has left them in the dust. Nine years later, they're trying to catch up to Domino's with Papa Track, their answer to the Pizza Tracker; but it's too little too late. They're sitting at the starting line coughing up dust while Domino's is off to the races.

Domino's figured out how to differentiate its offering with something more valuable than close-up images of melty cheese and empty platitudes like "Better ingredients. Better pizza." (Does anyone buy that Papa John's has superior ingredients and better pizza? Can they prove it?) Sadly, I've heard a lot of service contractors use a very similar line: "Better techs. Better service." Really? Do you think anyone is buying that? Even if they do, it's impossible to prove it's true, so why bother? Instead, take a page from Domino's book. Offer customers a better experience with service transparency and visibility.

Domino's technology creates value for the brand because it's focused on the customer experience as opposed to accounting and back-office operations. Everything they build is for the benefit of the customer. In some cases they even added administrative work for in-store employees to improve the digital outcome for the customer. Let me repeat that again: Domino's technological innovations for a better customer experience sometimes require *more* administrative work back in the kitchen. Let me explain.

The Domino's Pizza Tracker app is semi-automated, but Domino's employees still have to manually update the system to alert customers about the progress of their pizza. For example, every time a pizza is ready for the oven, an employee presses a button updating the status of that order. When the driver finishes packaging an order and heads for the car, a button is pressed by the driver to update the status again. These manual button presses happen for every order, whether or not the customer is actively using the Pizza Tracker. Domino's employees update the system just in case a customer decides to check on their order. With a sales volume of two million pizzas a day, that works out to almost one billion manual system updates a year. That's a lot of data entry! And for what? The customer. It's that simple.

Obviously Domino's has limited the cost of these billion customer updates substantially with a technology-enabled process. They're not picking up the phone and calling their customers multiple times per order to update them on progress; that would be ridiculously cost prohibitive, and it would annoy the customer. Yet that's exactly how most service contractors think about solving the same problem! "Better call the customer or send them an ad-hoc email to let them know what's going on with their service." That's an expensive approach.

Why not give every customer a great experience and let technology solve the problem by incorporating it into the typical workflow? For example, instead of techs calling, emailing, or texting to alert the office and customer that they are on the way to a service call, incorporate technology (like ServiceTrade's Service Link) that will, with a simple push of a button, log the tech's drive time, update the office staff, and send an en-route notification to the customer with a picture of the technician and the estimated time of arrival. Or, instead of signing a paper work order, waiting to get back to the office, scanning it, and emailing it to the customer with an ad-hoc summary and picture attachments, how about incorporating technology that automatically sends all this information to the customer the moment they sign the digital work order? Even if it adds a few new points of quick data entry, similar to Domino's button push, it shows the customer your company is taking care of them. This is the "impressions" part of MIPS (marketing *impressions* per service).

For Domino's, however, there were no cost savings with their new workflow. They weren't calling or emailing customers to update them on their orders in the first place, so these billion data-entry points were a net new expense. Despite that, they don't even think twice about the cost because they understand the value of *marketing impressions per service*, or MIPS.

MIPS is the heart and soul of Domino's customer-experience strategy. For each service (or pizza) delivered, a series of useful notifications is sent to the customer updating them on their purchase. In Domino's case, the customer receives push notifications (the little pop-up alerts generated by an app on your smartphone) on their mobile device throughout the delivery cycle. From prep to bake to delivery, they are notified about every step, and each notification links back to the Pizza Tracker, the visual manifestation of MIPS.

When you order a pizza for an office full of hungry coworkers or a house full of famished kids, you want certainty about your order. Hangry and anxious, they'll look to you for one answer: When will the pizza arrive? You can either be a zero or a hero. If you're in the dark and you leave your compadres in limbo, the anxiety will escalate and you're going to be a zero. Compare that to the certainty of "it just got boxed up and should be here in twelve minutes." That's more like it! You'll be the hero.

The next time you want a pizza, who are you going to call – the company that made you a zero or the one that gave you certainty and made you a hero? When your customer has failing equipment or systems in their building that impact their tenants, customers, or coworkers, who do you think they'd rather be – the zero or the hero? This doesn't apply just to emergency service work. For standard maintenance and inspections, they would also prefer to be certain about what's going on so they can keep their colleagues up to date, make arrangements on their end, and have peace of mind about the work being performed.

At the end of the day, what facility owners and managers really want is certainty. Strategically, that means certainty about their facility budget; tactically, that means certainty about the facility services they receive from day to day. They want certainty about everything from when the tech will arrive to how they should resolve equipment issues. MIPS give your customers *tactical* certainty by giving them the information they need to make good decisions on a service-by-service basis, and that builds trust that you can provide *strategic* certainty for their long-term goals. Service certainty can distinguish you from the unpredictable, unreliable competition.

MIPS Are Everywhere

From Amazon to Uber, MIPS are so ubiquitous that you might not even notice them anymore. Do you notice all the notifications you receive from Uber or Lyft for a single ride? Pay attention next time and see if you can count four or more. Do you ever think twice about the status updates you get from Amazon about your orders? "Your package has arrived!" I love that one. As a matter of fact, Amazon has a total of six MIPS during the order cycle. There are the obvious MIPS: 1) order confirmation, 2) order shipped, and 3) shipment arrival; but there are three more that Amazon uses to engage the customer to consider additional purchases and to help others make purchasing decisions.

When you're on the cusp of making a purchase, Amazon knows you are considering a product based on your browsing history on their website. You often receive an email offering an incentive to buy a product you have reviewed online or placed in your shopping cart. That's the fourth MIP associated with your buying cycle. Number five is the review request you receive after you have had some time to experience the product you purchased. Your review is one of the stories that might influence another prospective customer to purchase a product. Finally, number six in the Amazon MIPS cycle is a list of recommended products based on your recent purchase history. These recommendations are generated from data Amazon analyzes to discover trends in buying behavior. Ideally the data-driven recommendations feel like thoughtful advice from a shopping assistant to help you get the most value from your other purchases.

It's not just Amazon and other retailers that are using MIPS to drive product purchases. Think about the last time you caught a commercial flight. Did you receive any emails or texts from the airline with useful information about your flight? I know I have. In fact, one marketing impression from WOW air saved my vacation to Iceland in 2016. My wife and I travel abroad almost every year, so we understand the ins and outs of international travel. We usually do some quick research and a couple visa forms and we're good to go. That time we completely forgot. Had it not been for one of the airline MIPS reminding us to complete our APIS and ESTA authorizations, which had to be completed weeks in advance of our trip, we would have had to cancel our trip. MIPS saved our vacation!

At this point you're probably questioning what these *impressions* have to do with marketing when they all seem like customer service touches. MIPS are great customer service, but they earn the "marketing" label because they extend a digital wrap by reinforcing brand value and collecting online reviews. Take a look at some of the marketing impressions you've received from Amazon, Uber, or an airline. Notice their logo and brand identity in every single message? These are not plain-text emails from a random employee. On the contrary, when you receive one of these helpful notifications, these companies make certain the brand image and value is reinforced with every impression.

After the service is rendered or product delivered, practically every company employing MIPS asks for an online review. Reviews are the modern currency of trust. Without them potential buyers question the quality of services and products. For service contractors, this was only true for residential providers in the past. But times have changed. Commercial and industrial service contractors are benefiting from (or suffering from) online reviews (or the lack thereof).

Consumer companies like Domino's, Amazon, Uber, and airlines have all mastered the art of MIPS. They understand that the customer experience goes far beyond the moment a service is rendered. Leading up to and following delivery, there are ample opportunities to provide more actionable information in ways that reinforce their brand value. Though many of these communications don't seem like marketing in the traditional sense, they represent the future of branding via digital marketing for service contractors. They are not blatant, in-your-face promotions; instead they are seamlessly integrated into the service experience in a way that provides value to your customer and, therefore, builds value for your brand.

What's Your MIPS Number?

Below is a list of eight MIPS every service contractor should implement. Each communication serves a different purpose, but they are all similar in their form. Each one should be formatted to include:

- **Branding:** Always include your logo and company name in every communication.

- **Contact information:** Provide the most relevant point of contact for each type of communication.
- **Link to service details:** Much like the notifications sent by Domino's, your MIPS communications should include a link to additional details about the service(s) you are providing. Domino's links users to their real-time Pizza Tracker. Similarly, you should send users to a job summary like ServiceTrade's Service Link.

Now that you have the common format and content strategy, here are your unique MIPS opportunities:

1. Due-for-service reminder

Especially when providing relatively infrequent recurring services such as preventative/planned maintenance, inspections, and cleanings that occur less than monthly, a reminder that the customer is due for a service should be sent about a month before the service is actually due. This reminder helps you retain your position as the vendor of choice between services. Without it, the customer might turn to one of your competitors when they need service and your brand was not there to help. In addition to the format discussed above, this message should include:

- When the service is due
- What to expect next; for example, they will receive a call or email to schedule the service

2. Appointment reminder

Every appointment for a service should be preceded by an appointment reminder one to seven days in advance. Like the text reminder your dentist likely sends you before your teeth cleaning, this type of reminder is very helpful for the customer and reinforces that your brand is helpful, easy to work with, and technologically savvy. Include the following in this message:

- All upcoming appointment dates and times
- The technician's name, picture, and contact information
- Information about how to change appointment dates or times

3. Tech on the way

Much like Amazon's out-for-delivery notification, your tech should let your customer know that they are on the way and when to expect them. Customers appreciate the heads-up so they can prepare for the tech's arrival. This message should include:

- Expected arrival time
- The technician's name, picture, and contact information

4. Appointment complete

After the work is complete, the customer should receive a brief summary that provides access to pictures, videos, and other data that the technician collected during the appointment. Visibility to the great work your company provides builds trust and customer loyalty. The following should be included in this message:

- The time the appointment was completed
- The technician's name, picture, and contact information
- Any problems found
- Any recommendations for additional work
- A signed acknowledgment of work completed

5. Satisfaction survey and/or review request

Checking the pulse of your customer satisfaction is critical in building a dominant brand. If your customer satisfaction is high, take advantage of it by requesting an online review that can help grow inbound lead generation. This is a tricky situation, however, because you want to avoid bad reviews, but you also want the ability to correct a poor customer service situation. One approach is to only request reviews from customers who respond positively to a dynamic survey via a platform like SurveyMonkey or Google Forms. For example, if a customer indicates that they are happy, you can request a review on your Google My Business page. Another option is to use something like ServiceTrade's Service Reviews feature to generate reviews on your website that drive local search engine optimization.

However, your techs need to be savvy enough to *not* request a review when they fouled up on the service call. Foul-ups happen, and you should use them as opportunities to recover gracefully; but they *do not* represent review opportunities! Note also that you will likely receive a better review before you send an invoice to the customer, so be timely with the review request so that their response is delivered while your value is fresh in their mind and they are not yet focused on the invoice details.

6. Job summary

After the job is complete and your office personnel have had a chance to review and collate all the data gathered, a message should be sent to the customer summarizing what happened. Like the "appointment complete" MIPS, this message should provide the customer with visibility to the service(s) you provided using rich media like pictures, videos, and other data, in order to build trust and loyalty. Include the following:

- The dates and times all appointments were completed
- The technician's name, picture, and contact information
- Information about problems found
- Recommendations for additional work
- A signed acknowledgment of work completed

7. Invoice with job summary

In order to keep the primary focus on payment, this message should be limited to the most important details but still provide access to all the job information. Simplifying the payment process further reinforces that your brand is easy to work with. This message should include:

- An invoice file with details for payment, or, preferably, a link to view and pay the invoice online
- Payment due date

8. Personalized recommendations

This often takes the form of a quote for additional work for issues found by the technician. When a quote is sent within 48 hours of the initial service, the likelihood that a customer will approve new work increases dramatically. This message can be sent prior to the invoice if it is ready. It should include:

- Details of recommended services with access to general information such as a web page or video
- A link to an electronic quote with related pictures of the deficiency to make the situation more real and understandable for the customer
- An "approve now" button. For a great example, check out ServiceTrade's quoting feature.

You won't get money for nothing if your customers think all they get with your service is aggravation, uncertainty, and invoices. MIPS tell your customers the story of every service you provide and reinforce your value throughout the service cycle. Just like Domino's, you can keep your customers informed and give them a superior customer experience that illustrates how you are different from and better than your competition. Give them the certainty they need to trust that you are the premium provider.

In the next chapter we help you decide how you want to be different from your competition – in a good way! If you are going to charge a premium price, you have to be different. The examples we provide and the exercises we outline will give you confidence in your decision to be different in ways that are meaningful to your customers.

CHAPTER 5

SHAWN SAYS, "WHO DO YOU THINK YOU ARE? IF YOU DON'T KNOW, YOUR CUSTOMERS DON'T KNOW EITHER."

Conformity is the jailer of freedom and the enemy of growth.
— John F. Kennedy

The things that make me different are the things that make me.
— Winnie-the-Pooh

Sometimes being committed to your unique value proposition leads to difficult conversations with customers and prospects. Being different certainly helps your company stand out relative to the competition, but it can also feel pretty uncomfortable at times. I recall a customer visit that illustrates just how difficult it can be when you are committed to being different. Billy and I were visiting with Randy and Rebekah Akins, the owners of Aztec Fire and Safety in San Diego. Randy joined the meeting on the phone because he could not get to the office that day for some reason, and Billy, Rebekah, and I were sitting in Rebekah's office. Randy led off the conversation with why he had abandoned his last customer service platform and selected ServiceTrade. "The last application we used really screwed up our QuickBooks, and the most important thing ServiceTrade can get right is an elegant integration with QuickBooks," Randy declared through the phone speaker.

Uh oh, I thought to myself. *This is about to get really interesting.* Billy didn't let that comment go as I hoped he might. Favoring accounting productivity over great customer service is one of Billy's hot-button topics. Randy had just signed up with ServiceTrade the week before, and I guess Billy was pretty confident that Randy had already written and mailed the check because his first response was a verbal punch in the mouth for Randy: "Well then, you're likely to be disappointed with ServiceTrade if an elegant QuickBooks integration is what is most important to you. We focus most of our R&D spending on innovations that help you make more money from your customers through great customer service. We believe making more money and great customer service are far more important than how you send the information to your accounting application."

Billy had wasted no time getting to the heart of the conflict, and Rebekah and I stared awkwardly at each other wondering what was going to happen next. I was happy that Randy was not in the room because he seemed to be spoiling for a fight after wasting a year or more on an application and then switching to ServiceTrade to solve what he felt was his most important problem – QuickBooks integration. "That's a pretty arrogant thing to declare in a first meeting with a new customer. Basically you're telling me that what I want is not important and that you guys know better than the customer. We're going to be very disappointed if you can't help us with this QuickBooks problem."

Randy wasn't backing down either. I felt I should do something, but it was like watching a train wreck, and I felt paralyzed. I literally couldn't speak or move. Billy continued with, "We certainly don't mean to be arrogant, and you guys are important to us. I hope the QuickBooks thing works, but it might not. If you stick with us, however, I can promise you that in six months you will be thrilled with how much easier it is to take care of your customers, deliver more services, raise your prices, and attract new customers."

"We have already written the check, and we plan to make every attempt to be a good customer. I hope you're right because our last experience with technology was a huge disappointment." Randy closed the door on the fight, and we moved on to more comfortable ground with a conversation regarding the training and data-migration plan for Aztec.

Fast-forward eight months, and Billy and Randy are fast friends. Billy even attends Randy's kids' baseball games when he's in San Diego. Randy and Rebekah's business is growing like crazy, and they feel like ServiceTrade has made them stand out in their market. They are selling more services, raising prices, and attracting new and better customers to their brand. Billy took a calculated risk in that first conversation because he knew that the best ServiceTrade could do regarding QuickBooks integration was not going to impress anyone. QuickBooks is a low-cost, basic accounting application that is easy to use, but it has severe limitations regarding how third-party applications interface with it. There are no *application programming interfaces* (APIs) for the desktop version. (See chapter 8 for more about APIs.) Besides, being great at QuickBooks integration is not what sets ServiceTrade apart in the market. We know who we are as a company, and our mission is to help commercial service contractors use technology to deliver amazing customer service and become more valuable to their customers. QuickBooks specifically, and accounting generally, have no bearing on that mission.

Do you know who you are as a business? Do you know what makes you different and special in your market? Do your customers know who you are? Are you committed to being different even if it means being uncomfortable in your early engagements with customers and prospects who have learned bad habits from your low-end competition?

I love asking business owners and managers "Who do you think you are?" I'm not trying to pick a fight. What I'm really asking is "What's your brand promise and how does it make you different from and better than your competition?" But that's a pretty boring question. Those who can give me a concise, thoughtful answer generally run growing and profitable companies. Those who can't, don't. See if you can answer these questions about big consumer brands that advertise to you every day:

- What's Geico's slogan?
- What's Jimmy John's known for?
- What does BMW sell?

Think about these for a second. If you don't know the answers, you probably don't watch much TV. Geico's slogan is "15 minutes could save you 15% or more on car insurance." Jimmy John's is known for service that is "freaky fast." BMW sells "the ultimate driving machine." Even if you're not one of their customers, you've probably heard these brand promises before. That type of brand identity and awareness is powerful! Most people can easily recall these brand promises because these companies reinforce their position in the market over and over and over again with consistent and differentiated messaging. And they're not just empty promises; fulfilling these promises is what makes these brands different from and better than their competition.

These megabrands have spent gobs of money on television advertising to implant those promises in your head, but you are certainly not going to use their consumer advertising strategy for your commercial service company. Your digital wrap can accomplish the same brand awareness for your customers and prospects for much less money than television advertising. The more difficult and more important part is figuring out who you are. What is your brand promise? What makes you different from and better than your competition? I ask again, who do you think you are?

Let me guess. You have better techs so you can deliver better service? You care more? You work harder? Every commercial service contractor in your market says those things. I want to know what makes you different and better, not what makes you the same as everyone else. Don't worry – most companies never figure this out. And therein lies your opportunity. Discover what makes you different, commit to the customer segment that values your uniqueness, and you can earn a brand premium, also known as money for nothing. That's what we did at ServiceTrade.

Three years. That's how long it took us at ServiceTrade to figure out who we were and who we still are. In the software world, that's an eternity. It's not that we didn't have brand stuff. We had logos, a website, sales materials, a trade show booth, and more. On top of that we sold a lot of software. Anyone who had technicians in the field needed ServiceTrade! Like shooting fish in a barrel;

everything from towing companies to horse farriers – we sold it all. We even sold ServiceTrade to a dog food delivery company. Why not? They had people in the field who needed to be managed in order to maximize dog food delivery productivity. The problem, as it turned out, is that dog food delivery companies have very different needs from home service companies, who have different needs from commercial service contractors. Our customers all had different pain points, and we weren't doing a great job of solving them for anyone in particular. We inevitably lost lots of customers, which really sucked. In the software industry, customer *churn* is an unforgivable business sin. If you don't retain at least 95 percent of your revenue from existing customers, investors get very nervous. (See chapter 7 for more about churn.)

On top of high customer churn, the competitive landscape was getting very crowded. Our sales slowed down because prospective customers were choosing low-cost alternatives and competitors who offered features that were better suited to their industry. The last time I checked there were over 400 software products that made similar claims to those being made by ServiceTrade. "We help you manage technicians in the field!" proclaimed every website from these hundreds of upstart companies. How generic is that? "Field service management software." That's about as descriptive as a "fire protection company" or "mechanical service contractor."

What markets do you serve? How are you different from your hundreds of competitors? What makes you better? If you aren't any different, then you're selling a commodity. When you sell a commodity, all customers care about is price. When you compete on price, growing is tough and building a premium brand is impossible.

So there we were, selling a commodity in a sea of competitors selling the same thing. We were indistinguishable and undifferentiated. We thrashed around aimlessly for a few months until something finally clicked. We noticed that a segment of our customers was extremely happy with ServiceTrade because we were helping them grow their businesses. More specifically, our product and its features were a great fit for commercial service contractors because it helped them sell more contracts, be more productive, and deliver amazing customer service. Great news, right? Sort of. We had found a niche, but this niche represented only a tiny fraction of the overall market. Imagine that conversation with investors: "You want to pivot the entire company to pursue a market that's a tenth the size because you can't outsell the competition?" Yeah, that's an uncomfortable conversation.

Holed up in a cabin deep in the Appalachian mountains of North Carolina, our founding team faced the biggest decision the company has ever made. Billy, Brian Smithwick, James Jordan, Anna McMahon, and I tried to figure out whether or not we wanted to pivot the company to focus on serving a small fraction of the total market. The future of the company, our careers, and our coworkers' jobs were on the line. After two days of intense debate, we came up with a brand promise in the form of a mission statement:

> Help commercial service contractors use technology to
> become more valuable to their customers and
> grow their business.

As soon as we got back from the mountain retreat, we got to work. We completely changed our messaging, updated our website, purged our prospect database of leads that weren't fits, and cancelled trade show appearances. We even cancelled deals that were in progress because we didn't think the prospects were good fits for our new strategy. We were on a mission.

Adjusting our target market to focus on commercial service contractors was just the start. Our goal was to help our customers use technology to be more valuable to their customers and grow their businesses. That meant prioritizing our R&D budget on features that would help our customers make more money. While our competition focused on back-office efficiency and better integration with accounting applications, we doubled down on customer engagement features like online quoting and the ServicePortal where customers access job history and information about future work. These features made us different, and they also made us more attractive to the market we were targeting – but not to everyone. The commitment to being different led to more uncomfortable conversations like the one with Randy and Rebekah from Aztec Fire.

How do you decide which customers are the important ones and how to be different and special to them? There is no right answer to this challenge. Instead there is a set of commitments your company can make based on who you want to serve and how you intend to be different. Below I describe a simple exercise you can do with your team to help define who you want to be. I call the exercise "One Positive, One Negative."

The point of reviewing a positive and a negative about any dimension of your business is to draw a contrast that helps clarify the boundaries of your vision. Start by imagining a date five years from today. On that date you and your team members overhear some conversations. The first conversation is between a long-term customer of your company, "Aardvark Services," and a prospective customer who has no experience with your services. The prospective customer asks the long-term customer, "Tell me one positive thing about doing business with Aardvark Services, and also one negative thing you don't like." Have each of your team members write down short answers for both the positive and negative parts of the question. If this were an exercise about ServiceTrade, the two answers I would provide are:

Positive: If you have an idea regarding a feature to help you sell or deliver better customer service, they will probably deliver it before you can finish describing it.

Negative: If you want them to help you integrate more closely with your server-based accounting application, you will get a very short answer from ServiceTrade: "Here is our API documentation; have a nice day."

Focusing on our stated mission rather than on accounting integration helps us prioritize where we spend our innovation budget. It also helps us attract customers who want to grow instead of grind. Growing businesses are usually willing to spend more money on innovation than those that are grinding away at cutting expenses to lift the bottom line, which is a further incentive for ServiceTrade to choose growing customers. We made a conscious choice about our brand and what makes us special, and we channel all of our resources to live up to that commitment.

Let's imagine the same conversation between two customers of Jimmy John's sandwich shop. Remember Jimmy John's slogan? Freaky fast delivery. Here we go:

Positive: If you're in a hurry, you can get a sandwich at their store or delivered to your office practically before you finish placing the order.

Negative: I hope you like provolone cheese, because they do not offer cheddar, muenster, Swiss, American, or any cheese other than provolone.

Jimmy John's is so focused on being "freaky fast" that they have eliminated customer choice to streamline the order and sandwich-making process. For example, they only offer provolone cheese – no Swiss, no cheddar, no muenster, no American. It takes too long to manage the order and make the sandwich if they provide options. This trade-off is a no-brainer for Jimmy John's because it reinforces their "freaky fast" brand value with customers.

Now let's imagine a conversation five years in the future between two competitors of your company during lunch at a trade show. They are your competitors, so a response that is positive for them is negative for you. Here are the responses if the exercise were about ServiceTrade:

Positive: I get all the business I want when we are selling to the cable company, the utility company, a manufacturer, or a residential contractor.

Negative: If the company you are selling to is a commercial fire and safety contractor or a mechanical contractor, you better hope they haven't heard of ServiceTrade before you close the deal. ServiceTrade is ruthless when it comes to protecting their target market from us.

As I indicated above, ServiceTrade made a decision to sell only to commercial service contractors. We shrank the potential market size that we can serve by 90 percent, but we became very good at making our customers happy with our focused innovations. We also fight like hell to never let one get away, because each one is very precious to us.

Repeat this positive/negative exercise a third time by imagining a conversation between a long-term employee and someone considering a job at your company. The perspective of employees regarding the positives and negatives at your company reinforces your brand when their experience is aligned with your market promises.

Finally, have each team member identify one great customer you really enjoy and one who is a total pain in the ass. This gets to the heart of who you think you are. Don't focus on profit as the metric that matters. Ideally it is not a conversation about personalities either. Serving customers who really *appreciate* your company is very rewarding – it creates a positive vibe in the company. If you are good at your business and your customers really like your service, you will find a way to make money. Conversely, it doesn't matter how much profit you make from a customer who doesn't appreciate your value; eventually that relationship will cease because people will not tolerate being miserable over a long period of time just for money.

I'm not going to provide a ServiceTrade positive and negative to protect our innocent customer who was mostly a pain in the ass because we were not well suited to be important to them. You can handle this one quite easily on your own without an example, and I'm willing to bet that your team members quickly reach the same conclusions about who is a good customer and who is generally a pain in the ass.

There is a saying often attributed to Confucius, the ancient Chinese teacher and philosopher:

Choose a job you love,
and you will never have to work a day in your life.

Well, here is the money-for-nothing corollary to the wisdom of Confucius:

Choose customers who love what you do,
and you will earn more pay for less work because you can
charge a feel-good premium.

Now that you have figured out how to answer the question "Who do you think you are?" the next chapter focuses on showing your customer what makes you different during the sales cycle. When they can see how committed you are to innovations that define your unique value, it becomes easier to sell your premium program.

CHAPTER 6

TELLIN' AIN'T SELLIN'; EVERY CUSTOMER IS FROM MISSOURI, SO SHOW THEM SOMETHING!

Frothy eloquence neither convinces nor satisfies me.
I'm from Missouri. You've got to show me.
— Missouri Congressman Willard Duncan Vandiver

When your salespeople call on customers, what are they pitching? What do they present when they get that rare opportunity to show a high-profile prospect the benefits of working with your company? While I have not often been in the room when a commercial service contractor is pitching a customer, I have seen hundreds of websites for these companies, and I have been to lots of trade shows where they are exhibiting. I am generally not impressed by what I have seen, which is usually some version of one or more of the following themes:

We Work Harder!
(It sucks to work harder than the other guy.)

We Care More!
(I'm not certain what sucks more –
working harder or caring more.)

Better Technicians Means Better Service!
(This is the Papa John's pizza pitch. We saw how that
ended in chapter 4. Not well.)

We're a Family Business!
(The mafia is a family business, too.)

We've Been in Business a Long Time!
(Really? Why are you still such a small company?)

Sadly the website content for most commercial service contractors is typically a long and rambling word salad that doesn't add up to much value for the customer. Google is usually not impressed either, as most rank pretty low for relevance in organic search results. I imagine the salespeople are equally unimpressed with the company strategy, so their pitch quickly devolves to price:

How much are you paying now? We'll get the work done, and it will be cheaper! Let's negotiate labor rates and the markup on parts! We will be there 24/7 when things go wrong! Call us anytime and we will fix your broken equipment by working around the clock until everything is good again!

Competing on price and some vague promises to work harder and care more and fix broken equipment 24/7 and be more family-oriented sucks. Why should the customer believe anything the sales representative is saying? How can the sales rep make a better impression and move the conversation to valuable outcomes and away from these meaningless promises?

Of course the most important thing the salesperson can do is ask questions and understand the goals of the buyer. They can also offer a premium program, but you can't expect the customer to buy based on the promises and platitudes of a sales rep. Tellin' ain't sellin'! Your salespeople should be able to show the customer the value of your brand by demonstrating how the program works. I am fond of declaring that all customers come from Missouri, which is known as the "Show-Me" state. If you can't show them the value, you will not sell them the program.

So what does a premium program look like? And how can you demonstrate it to the customer in a way that is meaningful to them? Let's have a look at some examples from other industries, as well as a unique example from a commercial mechanical engineering contractor, to gain insights into components you should consider:

Amazon Prime: Amazon offers a subscription program called Prime, and nearly 70 percent of US households are Prime members. Prime members pay $119 per year (at the time of this writing) in exchange for free two-day shipping; access to a library of movies, television shows, and music; and a free Kindle book every month, among other things. The most important thing Prime does, however, is put Amazon at the top of the heap when a subscriber considers how to buy the next bag of dog food, supplies for their kitchen pantry, or Christmas gifts for their friends: *I've already paid for Prime; I might as well benefit from the free, expedited shipping!*

The program helps keep the Amazon brand top-of-mind for future purchases, *and customers pay for this marketing trick through their subscription fees!* It's brilliant marketing by Amazon.

Amazon allows prospective customers to try Prime free for a month to experience its value because Amazon knows that all customers are from Missouri. The free trial *shows* the customer why Prime is valuable instead of just *telling* the customer that they will like it if they buy it.

BMW Ultimate Care: BMW is a premium automotive brand that delivers what they claim is "the ultimate driving machine." Ultimate Care is their premium maintenance program. You pay in advance, typically at the time of purchase when financing is also a part of the conversation. Ultimate Care provides unlimited service consistent with the manufacturer's recommended service plan. All parts and service required for recommended maintenance are included at a 30 percent discount. The program is only available at BMW dealership locations, so you will be taking the car to the dealership and wandering about reviewing all the latest offerings from BMW as your maintenance plan is delivered.

Once again, brilliant marketing. You pay in advance, so you will certainly use the service, which requires you to come to the dealership on a regular basis. No doubt you will get a loaner vehicle for any extended services, and it will be the latest model at the upper end of your price range. You pay in advance so that BMW can deliver a hassle-free experience and market their latest offerings to you on a regular basis.

Brandt STORM: Brandt is one of the largest mechanical and electrical contractors in Texas, and STORM is their hi-tech approach to data monitoring and analytics. S.T.O.R.M. stands for Service, Technology, Optimization, Retro-commissioning, and Monitoring. For a fast-growing segment of customers, when Brandt starts an HVAC systems maintenance relationship, they perform a top-to-bottom review of the equipment while installing monitoring technology to track and analyze key performance data. The focus is on critical elements for which failure would result in expensive disruptions. As part of Brandt's comprehensive service approach, the data collected supports a continuous process of systems assessment, collaborative prioritization, remediation, and validation of results. The customer receives regular communication and attention from Brandt engineers and technicians to sustain the intended operating parameters of their equipment and review the utility cost performance of their facility.

By using data to focus on predictive maintenance instead of reactive maintenance, Brandt can help drive down operating costs, enhance system performance, and provide service exactly when it's needed, which enables them to continuously remind clients of the value of the Brandt brand! These services help reduce the risk of full-coverage maintenance agreements by alerting Brandt to respond to system issues before they become equipment failures. Over time the customer becomes conditioned to accept that quotes for new equipment and upgrades are based on the data and that it's in their best interest to avoid performance disruptions that fall outside the scope of the service agreement.

So what are the lessons you should take from these examples? How can you initiate a branded program whereby customers subscribe to information that you manage so you can receive premium pay for less labor delivered? How do you show all of these customers from Missouri that you are sensitive to their need to see the value before they buy?

1. **Brand your program.** What is your version of Amazon Prime? What do you call it? Is it the focus of your sales pitch to the customer? Does the name have rhythm and rhyme? Is it catchy? Does it convey some meaning? Is it easy to remember? It's okay if the name is merely descriptive, but it's better if it has some ring to it or if it means something. Ideally the name helps the sales rep tell the story and get the conversation going with the customer, and also helps the customer remember your brand. A good name demonstrates your company's thoughtfulness in how you communicate your value.

2. **Show, don't tell.** Your salespeople need to be prepared to give a demonstration of the program. Amazon gives prospective Prime members a month of free Prime membership to try out all the benefits. Do your salespeople have a way to easily demonstrate your subscription program experience? Just like Amazon Prime's free 30-day trial, ServiceTrade's sales reps show our customers the story of the program through the online experience. The customer gets to experience all the online storytelling enabled by ServiceTrade through en-route notifications, online Service Links with photos and videos of their equipment and its current condition, and online Quote Links for recommended repairs or retrofits, and they get to review service history, review equipment status, and request new service from the contractor website. This capability makes for a much better sales presentation than a bunch of platitudes and promises about working harder or caring more or being family-oriented. Remember, all customers are from Missouri and they are not impressed by frothy eloquence. You have to show 'em!

3. **Promote the features.** Can you enumerate the features of your program? In a list? Spend some time thinking about the names of the features. In addition to periodic planned services, include things like guaranteed response on service calls and a preferred rate schedule for planned work and service calls on equipment covered by the program, along with a higher rate schedule for service calls on deficient equipment that does not qualify for the program. Maybe you should have a monitoring component that helps detect failure symptoms before failures become disruptive and expensive.

4. **Get money for nothing.** If the only time you send your customer an invoice is when you have a labor or parts line item to bill, guess what… they will assume your value is in the labor and parts instead of your program. The fewer invoices you send to the customer, the better. Ideally, have them pay annually in advance. It's better for you and cheaper for them. I suggest a 10 percent discount for annual payment in advance, 5 percent for quarterly in advance, and full price for monthly payments. All your planned maintenance and monitoring activities should be billed as a subscription with *minimal details related to materials and labor.* The only time such details should show on an invoice is for unplanned, unquoted work that is billed on a time-and-materials basis, and these expenses should ideally be a minimal part of your relationship with your most important customers.

5. **Offer a good contract.** Put in place a subscription program agreement, a rate schedule, and a service-level agreement. Good fences make good neighbors, and good contracts make good customers. Be ready to drive contract execution through technology like DocuSign or Adobe eSign.

If your contract reflects your program promise, and your sales representatives have done an effective job demonstrating that promise during the sales cycle, your customer will have no problem immediately signing a contract for a three-year or longer commitment.

None of these elements of a subscription program are rocket science, but it is surprising how rarely they are implemented by service contractors. Don't let shoddy practices in your industry or weak competitors who always sell on price dictate your business model. The executives of your company should spend at least 50 percent of their time working on program and marketing innovations that set your brand apart from competitors. Innovation rarely happens by accident, and it is the key to having a differentiated value proposition. Innovations are typically grounded in technology, but they can also take the form of unique ways to engage the market such as a subscription program for maintenance, monitoring, and inspections.

When innovations are bundled into a program that the sales team can sell for a premium price because it incorporates the principles above, you will discover over time that you are earning more pay for less work – money for nothing. In the next chapter we lay out a series of metrics you can use to measure your progress in building a market-leading, money-for-nothing brand.

CHAPTER 7

HOW MANY? HOW MUCH? HOW LONG?; TRACKING THE METRICS THAT MEASURE THE VALUE OF YOUR BRAND

All you need in this life is ignorance and confidence,
and then success is sure.
— Mark Twain

Bernie Madoff was arrested in 2008 for running what is believed to be the largest Ponzi scheme ever. Over a period of more than 20 years Madoff convinced wealthy, high-profile, private clients like Steven Spielberg and the Wilpon family (owners of the New York Mets), along with sophisticated commercial clients like MassMutual, Banco Santander, and HSBC, to entrust their money to his firm. The reason these folks went along with the scam is not because Madoff delivered eye-popping results with a brilliant strategy; he was not like John Paulson, who famously made over $4 billion in a period of less than 12 months by using credit default swaps to bet against the subprime mortgage lending market. Instead Madoff drew high-profile clients and sophisticated financial firms into his orbit by projecting modest but consistent returns.

Over a period of just over 14 years Madoff reported results that were marginally better than the return of the Standard and Poor's index, and over that very long horizon he reported a monthly loss only seven times. This extraordinary consistency led several financial forensics investigators to question Madoff's legitimacy, but the allure of consistent albeit modest positive returns was a powerful magnet for investors. They all turned a blind eye to the fraud while funneling enormous sums of money to Bernie.

The lesson for the service contractor is not that fraud is a good road; Bernie is serving a 150-year sentence for his crimes and the related $17.5 billion in losses he cost his clients. The lesson for the service contractor is that predictable, steady growth over a long period of time is an irresistible attraction for sophisticated investors. One day you will want an outsider to set a value for your business as part of an exit strategy or for the purpose of passing the business to a new generation. What metrics will you use to guide your efforts during the many years leading up to that valuation day? How can you deliver steady, market-beating results that aren't affected by the various dips and swings you inevitably experience while serving your customers? The key is to find a strategy that minimizes volatility and maximizes consistency over a long period. You need to deliver for real what Bernie falsely projected in order to impress those who will ultimately value your business.

In chapter 3 I described the efforts that Red Hat made to avoid a business model based on break/fix technical support. There were some very sophisticated investors on Red Hat's board of directors, and they knew that the volatility of break/fix was to be avoided. They helped steer the company toward a better strategy based on subscription services. During my time with DunnWell, the service contracting company that preceded ServiceTrade, I witnessed firsthand the difficulty of delivering steady, predictable income performance when the mix of services leans too heavily toward the break/fix model. One particular management meeting stands out in my mind. It was a March meeting to review the February results, and the tension between the steady, predictable outcomes of maintenance work and the more volatile break/fix outcomes became vividly clear.

February temperatures that year had been brutally cold throughout much of the country, and lots of sprinkler pipes had frozen at our customers' locations, even in the southern states. The emergency revenue was very high for that February because we responded to so many frozen pipe situations. Maintenance and planned-repair revenue, however, was somewhat lower than expected. Overall revenue exceeded our target by about 15 percent based on the strength of the emergency service calls. Gross margins were okay, but not what we expected when we had much higher revenue to absorb delivery costs. "Shouldn't the margins be higher since we charge more for emergency work?" I naively asked. "Nope," replied Sean McLaughlin, the head of operations. "We have to pay an arm and a leg to get people to respond to these emergency calls on a bitterly cold winter night. It is always a scramble. Costs are higher, and the administrative burden is also higher because you have to constantly field calls from the customers and then call them back with updates." Looking at the numbers, I guessed, "So the maintenance revenue is lower because our people were focused on chasing down problems instead of staying on top of the planned work?" Sean snorted, "That MIT education is paying real dividends for you right now, isn't it?"

During a typical month DunnWell delivered between 92 and 96 percent of contracted maintenance, inspection, and repair work. We called this measurement the "due versus done" ratio. It represented the amount of work delivered and invoiced divided by the total amount customers had authorized via maintenance contracts or approved repair quotes. To be strictly correct, it should have been called the "done versus due" ratio, but it was named before I got there, and "due versus done" had a better ring to it. That cold February, the "due versus done" ratio sagged downward to about 80 percent.

When that metric lagged, Joe Dunn, the largest shareholder in DunnWell, would complain to everyone that "the customer has written a check and laid it on the counter, and we couldn't be bothered to show up and cash it." Put in those terms, it seems pretty silly to let anything get in the way of cashing a check, but it was surprising how often people with good intentions could become distracted by chaos and neglect to pick up those checks. The distractions typically take the form of some emergency, and in the case of this cold February, the distraction was caused by frozen pipes and irate customers. But the February revenue was really good, and the overall margin was good, so what was the problem?

The problem was that not all margin dollars are equal. That sounds silly, but it's true. For this February period, DunnWell did not cash some checks for planned maintenance because we were busy cashing checks for emergency work. How do you suppose the customers who were due for planned maintenance felt when we did not show up as promised? How about the customers whose pipes burst? Do you suppose they were happy with the emergency response charges? And do you believe those emergency service dollars were going to show up consistently every February as contract maintenance dollars do? Not a chance.

Emergency service calls, by their very nature, are unpredictable – the opposite of consistent results. So even though revenue was higher and overall margins were acceptable, that cold February was a failure. Just because the gross margin on every job is in an acceptable range does not mean that the business is performing in a way that maximizes value for the owners. The emergency scramble gets in the way of the Bernie Madoff lesson that teaches us that consistency is better.

If revenue and service-call gross margin are not perfect measurements for management success, what are the measurements that matter? How can the owners of the business look back at the past month or quarter and make a judgment regarding success or failure? If the business is an investment it should be measured like an investment, and the investments that people value most highly are those that deliver predictable returns over and over again. Bernie Madoff famously played on this investor bias by cooking the books to show steady and consistent returns, no matter the market conditions, in order to lure more investors to his Ponzi scheme. Investors will always pay a premium for an investment with steady and consistent returns. So what are you going to measure to be certain you are optimizing for consistent and predictable returns?

Your business, just like an investment firm, faces uncertain market conditions. Instead of swings in the Dow Jones Industrial Average, the S&P 500, and the NASDAQ, you are dealing with cold weather, hot weather, fuel price fluctuations, tight labor markets, and swings in customer buying sentiment brought about by the same economic indicators that affect Wall Street. In the face of all of these potential distractions, you need a simple and effective formula to focus your team on the long-term measurements that matter so they can more effectively navigate a path through the occasional chaotic situation. Before I reveal the formula, see how you do at answering these questions:

- How many customers do you have under annual or longer maintenance contracts?
- What is the monthly recurring revenue (MRR) or annual recurring revenue (ARR) for these contract customers? This is the predictable maintenance, monitoring, and inspection revenue that always shows up on the income statement regardless of market conditions.
- What is the total contract value (TCV) of future committed revenue for maintenance, monitoring, and inspections for all customers under contract? Are your customers signing two-, three-, and four-year commitments to you?
- How many customers pay you in advance for your maintenance program? What is the amount of this deferred revenue on the balance sheet? If many of your customers are paying you in advance, it means you can use that cash to fund sales to new customers.
- What is the ratio of planned service revenue (maintenance, inspections, quoted repairs) to unplanned service revenue (emergency service calls to fix something that broke)? Higher ratios mean better customer service, and better customer service means customers will stick with your company for a longer term. Customers don't like unplanned expenses or the disruptions they represent.

- What is the net revenue churn in the customer base? How much revenue did you earn this year from customers who have been with you for over a year relative to the revenue from those same customers for the prior year? This ratio is ideally 90 percent or even higher. Minimal account churn means your digital wrap is sticky.

- What is your contract renewal rate? What percentage of customers does not renew their contract when it comes due? How much annual contract revenue on average do these non-renewing customers represent? These numbers represent your gross churn, and ideally gross churn should be less than 10 percent.

The answers to these questions are directly related to the value of any service business, yet not one of them mentions gross margin for service calls. That's important, but gross margin on contract maintenance, monitoring, inspections, and planned repairs is actually much more important. Predictable growth is even more important. No investor will complain about an occasional expense hiccup for unplanned services in the context of a highly predictable, growing stream of high-margin contract revenue. The very nature of unplanned repair work (it is unplanned!) makes it volatile and not particularly valuable to an investor, so optimizing gross margin on this work is the least of your concerns. Try to eliminate these disruptive emergency service calls altogether if you can.

I recognize that many of the questions above are kind of technical and difficult to absorb until you get into the swing of these measurements. So, as promised, I am going to give you a simple formula along with some advice to get you on the path of regularly measuring the growth in the value of your business. First let's talk about the simple formula I always reference as the driver of business value. It is three simple questions to ask over and over again:

How many? How much? How long?

These three questions underpin the basic value-building fundamentals for almost any business. How many? refers to how many customers are under contract to pay for services. It can also be how many locations or how many individual pieces of equipment are under contract. Ideally you measure all three: customers, locations, and equipment under contract. Any business that is overly reliant on a small number of customers, even if they are large customers, has higher risk associated with future income. A single screw-up or a management change at the customer can result in a major customer firing you for some random reason, wrecking your company. It is better to have many customers with many locations with lots of equipment so that the risk and volatility to revenue and margins is lower.

At the end of every quarter and every year, you should measure how many customers/locations/equipment-under-contract (simply "units" from here forward) were serviced that quarter compared to the same period the prior year. When looking at your quarterly results, ask these questions:

1. How many units are under contract now versus a year earlier? Is the number higher than last year?

2. How many units that received service last year did not receive service this year, whether because service was declined or they are no longer under contract?

3. How many new units did your company add through sales efforts? Count only those that are actually under contract. Is this number higher than the number you lost?

Here is a simple quarterly chart you can use to plot this information:

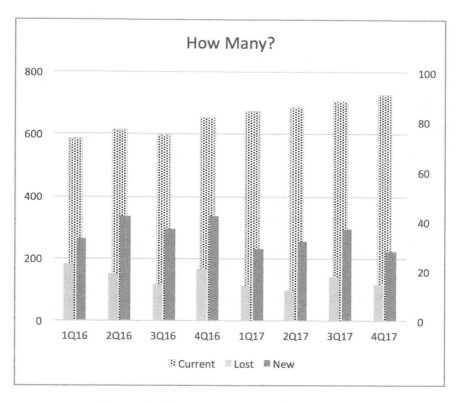

Figure 2: Customer units under contract
plus new sales and lost units

I like to measure the total units under contract on the left axis while measuring units won and lost on the right axis. This allows the comparison between won and lost to stand out, because those numbers may be relatively small when compared to the total number of units. Ideally the total grows nicely over a series of several quarters and the number of units won is significantly higher than those lost. If losses are higher than wins, you are experiencing *churn*. Churn is bad. It indicates that something is wrong with customer service, and it will decimate your business if you don't address it.

The second question in our business-value formula is How much? How much? refers to the amount of revenue you can collect for servicing a given unit. The higher the number the better, of course. There are generally two ways to drive this metric higher: 1) raise prices to charge more for what you do, and 2) do more for the customer. Investors love companies with pricing power in their markets. Companies that can raise prices without losing customers to the competition are valuable to shareholders. Customers love companies that can do more for them because having fewer vendors to manage is always better. It is also more difficult to replace a vendor that is doing many things, so your services are likely to be more durable in the face of an occasional customer service hiccup.

Every quarter you should measure the amount of revenue you earned from each unit relative to the amount of revenue you earned in the same quarter for the prior year. Were you able to raise prices? Did customers respond to your solicitations for larger amounts of their business? Did they buy new innovations or suggested upgrades that you recommended? Were you able to use the information gathered as part of your digital wrap to pull them into a deeper and broader business relationship?

I suggest that you group your units into "cohorts" that indicate what year (or quarter or month depending on how many units you regularly add) the service commitment for that unit was initiated. You can plot how much money you are getting each year from units you have serviced for one year, two years, three years, four years, and so forth. You will ideally grow the amount of sales for every cohort group for the first few years and then hold on to most of that business during subsequent years. Some churn after a number of years is understandable as customers go out of business, merge, change strategies, or experience other corporate disruptions that affect their relationships with you. However, if you can show strong growth in revenue from existing units along with staying power within accounts as a business pattern, a new investor will pay you a premium for that trend.

Here is a quarterly chart over a two-year period that shows how revenue breaks down by unit cohorts grouped into the year you landed the service contract for the unit.:

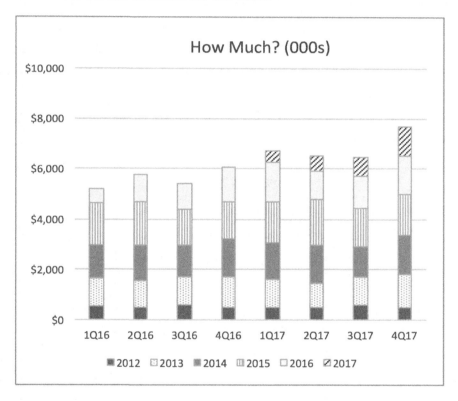

Figure 3: Revenue by annual period cohort group

Notice how the 2017 cohort started small but expanded over the course of the year. This pattern tells investors they can invest money in new sales efforts with the certainty that the customer count will grow over time and new customers will stick with your company for a long period after they experience your valuable program.

There is a second measurement for How much? that you should track for your management reviews. As indicated above, all revenue is not created equal. Emergency revenue is stressful, unpredictable, and unlikely to repeat. Group your revenue into three categories and measure how it evolves over time:

1. Category 1: Subscription program income
2. Category 2: Income from quoted work and planned retrofits, repairs, and upgrades delivered on a non-emergency basis for the long-term benefit of risk-free equipment performance
3. Category 3: Unplanned repairs such as emergency service calls; these services deliver the least valuable revenue and margin for your business

Here is a quarterly chart that shows the revenue breakout in your business for these three categories:

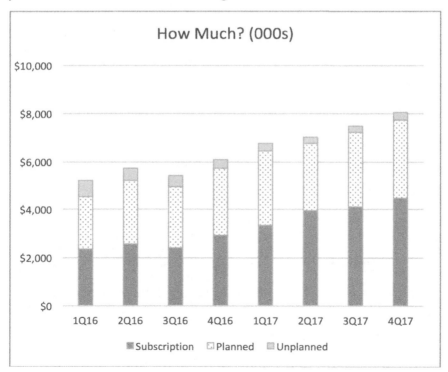

Figure 4: Revenue by service classification

You should generate this type of chart for all your larger customers individually as well to see how you are managing their business toward a predictable, low-risk relationship that is better for both you and them. You are ideally growing your revenue from contract maintenance, monitoring, inspections, planned repairs, and retrofits rather than emergency service calls. Emergency service calls usually stem from equipment malfunctions, which should decrease since you are monitoring and inspecting that equipment regularly. Planned work is more efficient and more scalable because the logistics can be meticulously coordinated. Customers benefit and your business benefits when you can plan the work to avoid excess travel time and overtime expenses, expedited parts shipping fees, and the general administrative stress associated with delivering service "right now." You can get customers' equipment assets under control and minimize service calls by quoting planned repairs to replace or upgrade equipment that is prone to failure with more robust equipment that is less likely to break down.

A commitment to minimize emergency work is a company value that you should stress during your sales pitches to customers. Here are a couple of graphic illustrations you can share with customers to make your point about the win-win nature of your premium management program:

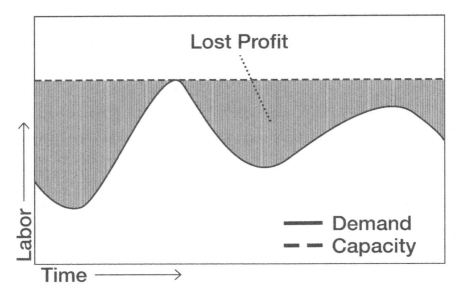

Figure 5: Highly variable demand, high capacity costs, and significant profit loss

The oscillating, sine-wave-shaped pattern in Figure 5 represents unfiltered demand associated with random equipment breakdowns when no subscription program is in effect across the customer base. The service capacity line represents the perfect customer service situation of being able to deliver a robust response to every random service call. Unfortunately scaling up for perfect response to peak demand means you lose lots of money as you keep that workforce in place during random slack periods. This is not an option for you.

Now let's look at the scenario in which you scale back your technician workforce to realize some profit by avoiding the high cost of having service technicians on the clock during slack periods.

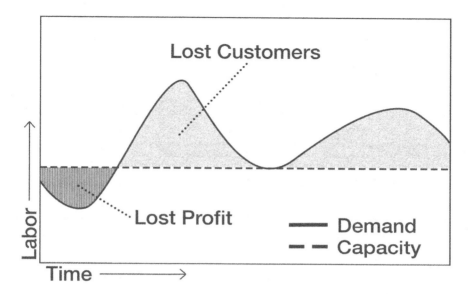

Figure 6: Highly variable demand, optimal capacity cost, and significant customer loss

In this scenario your business faces the twin perils of losing profits and losing customers. During peaks your lack of response will certainly lead to unhappy customers who are forced to find another service contractor. Since it is unlikely that you would ever staff at the absolute bottom of the demand curve, you are also still losing profit during low-demand periods when you have high labor carrying costs. These become more exaggerated as you lose customers because slack periods become more frequent and shallow. This scenario is a death spiral for the business.

The ideal situation is to get the customer demand curve under control on a customer-by-customer basis by putting customers into a subscription program that provides incentive for both you and them to eliminate the risks that ultimately drive equipment failure and unplanned, high-stress emergency service calls. Your goal is to minimize the amplitude of the fluctuations by minimizing equipment breakdowns.

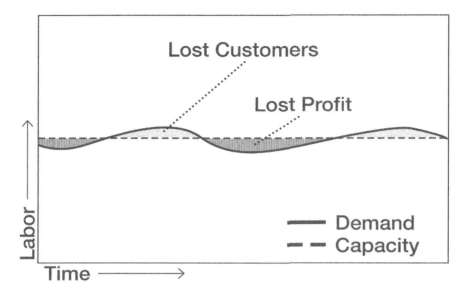

Figure 7: Minimal demand variation optimizes profit
and customer retention

In this scenario customers pay more for your subscription program, and in return they have less risk of failure and fewer unplanned expenses. The maintenance routine squishes down the amplitude of the failure modes to eliminate the twin inefficiencies of poor customer service during the peaks and poor profit performance during the valleys. If you do a good job demonstrating to them the story of their equipment via video and photo evidence, they will not have a problem with the cost of your subscription program because they can see that you really are working to optimize equipment performance. They will also generally accept your advice regarding repairs, retrofits, and upgrades that further eliminate risks, disruptions, and unplanned expenses when they can see the evidence of deterioration in photos and videos. The ideal situation, as always, is that you are getting money for nothing – no breakdowns and no disruptions – while the customer sees daily evidence through your digital wrap that they are indeed paying for "something" very valuable.

You should definitely share with customers the idea that you are trying to shape their demand curve in a way that minimizes the unplanned disruption of equipment failures and minimizes the share of your revenue that comes from emergency service calls. Show them the chart in Figure 4 above indicating the share of revenue from maintenance, monitoring, and planned repairs relative to emergency service calls. Show them customers similar to their profile for which your subscription program has shifted emergency-service spending to planned spending and lowered the overall cost to the customer. I bet sharing this data will help you build buy-in to your premium program.

Investors also love this type of analysis because they correctly assume that your subscription and quoted-work revenue is more stable and predictable than the unplanned services. Unplanned work is hard to predict, and it is also stressful on the organization. It represents a risk to both profit and customer satisfaction. Having this data readily available in a new-investor pitch demonstrates thoughtfulness in your approach to long-term, sustainable shareholder value.

Finally, the last measurement in our catchy shareholder-value jingle is How long? How long? refers to the duration of your relationship with a customer. If you can create a really sticky digital wrap that reinforces the story of your brand throughout the service cycle, you should in theory be able to hold on to those customers for a very long time. The chart that I like to use to demonstrate this metric is a simple column chart that shows total units under contract and how long you have maintained a contract for those units.:

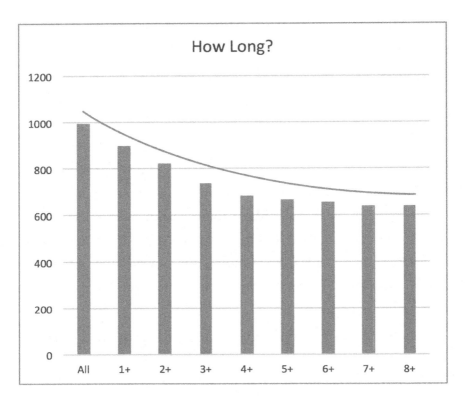

Figure 8: Customer retention over a long term

The curve at the top of the chart ideally flattens to a steady state pretty quickly after a couple of years, indicating that after an initial break-in period your customers stick with your company for a very long time.

Investors love sticky brands with repeat customers who pay up year after year in a predictable manner to continue receiving terrific results. They also love companies that can demonstrate they are able to attract new customers and grow their business in a programmatic fashion. They are also just like customers in that they generally do not want to pay money for nothing. In this case "nothing" refers to a sales pitch with platitudes that ultimately add up to "Trust me! It's gonna be great!"

When you can show the story of How many? How much? and How long? with the charts provided above, you will make potential investors feel good. When they feel good, you have earned the right to command a premium for the valuable business you have assembled. Show them the charts you use to measure the business value you are generating. I bet they are impressed, and you might be surprised at just how much money-for-nothing you get if you ever decide to sell shares in your company.

Clearly investors value a business that can show consistent growth over a long horizon, but employees also value growth. Over the next few chapters we review some ideas about how to evaluate technology investments relative to their growth potential, while also commenting on the intangible benefits of a culture that prioritizes growth. A growth culture, along with a couple of tricks oriented toward the career values of millennials, helps you attract talented employees and keep them for the long haul.

CHAPTER 8

APPLYING THE BANK BANDIT TEST FOR TECHNOLOGY INVESTMENTS

That's where the money is!
— Slick Willie Sutton's response to a reporter's question
about why he was fond of robbing banks

Slick Willie Sutton was a bank bandit who practiced his trade in the early 1900s. When a reporter asked Willie why he was so fond of robbing banks, he reportedly replied, "That's where the money is!" If the goal of robbery is money, banks are the obvious target. And if the goal of your business is making money, shouldn't you focus the maximum amount of time and investment, particularly for technology applications, on the obvious target of getting more money from customers?

Slick Willie liked to rob banks because they delivered more bang for his buck (or more bucks for his bang if Willie had to actually shoot it out) than robbing hotels or restaurants or retail merchants. Where is the money in your market? It's in the hands of your prospects and customers, and you should consider how to use technology to stick 'em up (in the friendliest way possible, of course!) and transfer more of their money to your bank account.

The idea of using technology as a weapon to get more money from customers is radical thinking for most service contractors. Instead of thinking like a bank bandit and investing in technology "guns" to take more money from customers and prospects, most are focused on shaking down the neighborhood kids' lemonade stand instead – the small percentage of payroll associated with administrative overhead. Like the neighborhood kids, this spending is a soft target – they do not resist much when executive management pounds the table demanding a chunk of expense flesh. Similar to the revenue of a neighborhood lemonade stand, however, administrative spending represents a miniscule amount of money. By definition, administrative spending is a small percentage of revenue – maybe 10 percent. Using technology to transfer a portion of this tiny spending to net income isn't going to increase the value of your business very much.

Contrast your administrative spending with the amount of money in the hands of customers and prospects in your market. These "banks" are holding on to 100 to 1,000 times your current revenue. They are going to spend it with someone, so why not use technology to stick 'em up and have them spend it with you? Slick Willie would do the obvious thing and forget about the lemonade stand and focus all his attention on the big pile of money being held by customers and prospects.

The reason most service contractors focus so intently on administrative overhead as a target for technology spending is because accounting and back-office applications are often the only technology applications they have ever purchased. Most are a bit behind in their thinking about technology. Salesforce.com and related sales, marketing, and customer service applications such as HubSpot, Marketo, and ServiceNow have been the fastest growing category of enterprise applications over the past 10 years. If you have ignored these changes in the market, don't be too alarmed. The fact that you're reading this book probably puts you in the top 10 percent of growth-oriented service contractors looking for an advantage in the market. You just need some guidelines on how to spend your technology budget to be more like Slick Willie Sutton.

In chapter 9 of *The Digital Wrap* we covered how to research and buy good applications. We did not, however, provide any guidelines on how to think about the value of those applications to your business, so we are going to focus on that in this chapter. But before we move on to Slick Willie's advice for technology, it is worth revisiting one highlight from *The Digital Wrap* regarding the most simple and basic test for determining if an application you are considering is worth at least one penny, or if it is worth nothing. Even if it's free, you should not consider any application that does not pass the following test. Go to your favorite online search engine and enter this search query:

"[name of software application] API documentation"

The first organic entry below the advertisements with "Ad" in the little boxes to the left of the links should be a site maintained by the vendor of the application in question. That site, if it exists, provides detailed documentation regarding how the application you are considering can be integrated with other applications you use. Application programming interfaces (APIs) are the key to a new world of connected innovations for your business. Without good, publicly documented APIs, the application you are considering is worthless. You should not pay anything for it. If you cannot easily find this documentation with the simple search above, do not even consider buying the application in question.

APIs are critically important because you are going to be buying many applications. There is no such thing as an "all in one" application. The idea that any single vendor with a single application can handle all the technology requirements for your business is a silly idea, and any vendor making that promise is a silly vendor. If you are going to buy many applications, those applications must work seamlessly together. The best developers of the best applications all use APIs as the basis for their scalable development processes. If those APIs do not exist, the developers are not high-quality professionals, and the applications they deliver will be clunky, difficult to use, and impossible to integrate with other interesting applications that you might want to enjoy.

Try the search above for a couple of quality applications that are on the market today. Insert "ServiceTrade" or "ZenDesk" or "PipeDrive" or "Marketo" or "Hubspot" or "Slack" or "Salesforce" or "ServiceNow" and check out the first organic link to get an idea of what should be listed.

Let's say that your application passes that first test. What now? How much is it worth? What would Slick Willie do? It depends on how much the application increases the value of your business. In chapter 7 I argued that the questions that determine the value of your business are How many? How much? and How long? These all relate to how much money you can take from the maximum amount of customers in your market. These are also the fundamental questions you should use to evaluate how much a new software application is worth to your business. The more the application impacts these measurements, the more you should be willing to pay because it is going to make your business more valuable.

First use the following questions to measure the potential value of a new application. Does the application:

1. Help me attract new customers?
2. Make my brand stand out and give my salespeople something unique to talk about?
3. Enable me to charge customers a premium because it provides some cool new service features that customers value?
4. Give me a new service line to sell to customers that complements the other service lines I'm already selling?
5. Make my services sticky so that it is difficult for customers to fire me and replace my company with a low-cost competitor?
6. Make it more difficult for a customer to switch to a new vendor?

If the answer to one or more of these questions is "yes, absolutely, definitely," the application is probably very valuable. If the answer is "no, not really," the application might be worth something, but it's probably only worth a fraction of how much you would save by eliminating some administrative burden from the business. Determine how many people you can fire if the application eliminates the work they perform, and the associated payroll savings is the value of the new application to your company. That type of expense relief can be worthwhile, but, as indicated above in our lemonade-stand example, it's not nearly as valuable or fun as applications that drive more revenue and make customers more dependent on your company.

How much should you be willing to spend on technology to be more like Slick Willie? How much is technology that helps you rob the customer bank worth? How can you think more like a bank bandit when making technology decisions? To get a sense of how to value these decisions, let's look at some examples from ServiceTrade and how much we pay for technology that helps us take more money from more customers.

The biggest technology application expense that ServiceTrade faces is for technology that powers our customers' experiences with our products. Amazon and Google charge us for technology that provides cool features in our application. For example, with Quote Link our customers can send quotes to their customers via emails with links to an interactive web page that includes photos, videos, audios, and a "one click to approve" button to accept the quote proposal. This feature drives revenue for our customers and is largely dependent on capability provided to ServiceTrade by Amazon Web Services. And the ability to map customer locations for scheduling efficiency, see the locations of the technicians in real time, and prefill the fields for setting up new customer-location records is largely dependent on Google's map APIs. (There are those APIs again, delivering value from one great company to other great companies that use them!) The applications from Amazon and Google are *very* valuable to ServiceTrade because they help us attract new customers and charge them a premium. We spend about 6 percent of our revenue on these types of applications.

ServiceTrade makes about 80 percent gross margin on the applications we sell, so we can afford to spend heavily on applications from partners like Google and Amazon that enable cool features for our customers. If your gross margin for services is lower, say 35 percent, then spending 6 percent of revenue on any application doesn't make any sense at all. The proportionate comparison in this case is roughly 7 percent of gross margin, which would equal 2.6 percent of revenue for an application that really helps you deliver differentiated value to your customer. For a $10 million service contracting business generating 35 percent gross margin, the equivalent amount would be $260,000 per year. To scale this amount to your business, simply divide your service revenue by $10 million and multiply that number by $260,000.

The next biggest category of technology expense at ServiceTrade is for sales and marketing applications. We use Salesforce, Marketo, SalesLoft, and a handful of other applications that help us present our value proposition to customer prospects in ways that drives new sales. These applications help us increase the How many? metrics associated with new customers. We spend about 1.5 percent of revenue on these types of applications. Again, to adjust for gross margin, that would be about .6 percent of revenue for a 35 percent gross margin business. For a $10 million service contracting business with 35 percent gross margin, the equivalent annual expense would be $60,000.

The next biggest category of technology expense at ServiceTrade is for customer-service-oriented applications. These are the applications that help our engineers and support staff keep track of and respond to customer service requests and monitor the application for errors or potential signs of trouble. We spend about .4 percent of revenue on these types of applications. They are tangentially oriented toward helping with the How long? metrics that measure how long our customers stick with ServiceTrade in the face of the myriad low-cost competitors in the market. Clearly these are far less valuable to us than Google and Amazon, and also less valuable than the sales and marketing applications, both of which help us drive up the How many? and How much? elements of our business value. Adjust for gross margin again, and you get .16 as the percentage of revenue in a 35 percent gross margin business. A $10 million service contracting business should consider spending $16,000 per year on customer service infrastructure.

Finally there are the administrative applications like accounting, email, file-sharing, calendar, reporting, office productivity, etc. These are applications that every business needs, but their value is simply in keeping the administrative burden of running a tight ship as low as possible. ServiceTrade spends about .3 percent of revenue on these types of applications. For a $10 million service contracting company generating 35 percent gross margin, spending for administrative applications should be on the order of .13 percent of revenue, or about $13,000 per year.

If we total all these for a $10 million service contracting business, the percentage of revenue spent on technology applications is about 3.5 percent of revenue, or about $350,000 per year. My ears are almost bleeding from the screams and bellows of "That's crazy!" that I can hear coming from service contracting customers reacting to this number. But is it crazy? Are applications that help your business become more competitive at attracting new customers, driving new revenue, and charging a premium price really worth that type of spending?

Here is another way to think about how to value technology and benchmark these numbers against other applications that might be more familiar to you. As the quote from Slick Willie Sutton at the beginning of the chapter illustrates, it is easy to invest in activities that are directly related to the money you want to collect. While most commercial contractors never deal with collections in the field, there are some cases in which certain customers must be handled on a COD basis due to their poor credit situation. How much do you pay for an application like Square that helps you collect money from a COD customer in the field? Square helps consummate the sale by getting the cash now, and you happily pay about 2.5 percent of revenue for this type of collection application. It is close to the money, so it is easy to justify the expense using the Slick Willie investment logic.

Consider how much retail merchants pay to folks like Amazon and eBay to market their goods and streamline conversion of a prospect to a buying customer. The going rate is about 10 percent of the value of the sale for these platforms; when you buy from a third-party merchant on Amazon or eBay, the technology platform provider keeps about 10 percent of the sales price. If technology helps you steer valuable prospects to your brand and turn them into valuable customers who pay for your services over many years, maybe that technology can command as much as 10 percent of the first year transaction value, similar to the amount that Amazon and eBay charge to retail merchants for customer conversion.

If you are in the fire safety or security field, you might be selling a monitoring service to your customers. How much do you pay for the central station monitoring application that enables you to sell high-margin monitoring? I bet you happily pay between 30 and 50 percent of revenue for this valuable addition to your service arsenal. Monitoring is a high-margin, high-value revenue stream that differentiates your service offering, and 30 to 50 percent of revenue is much higher than the 3.5 percent benchmark we derived from my analysis above. Applications that drive high-margin revenue growth are easily worth a premium relative to back-office applications.

The problem with the 3.5 percent benchmark is that you are probably already significantly overpaying for administrative applications like accounting and underinvesting in applications that drive new-customer acquisition, service differentiation, and revenue. I am willing to bet that most of the application purchases you have made in the last 10 years score low on the "bank bandit" test. I am also willing to bet that your accounting application provider is telling you, "We have a plugin for sales, and customer service, and technician management, and marketing, and human resources, and every other thing you might need," in order to justify the crazy price you are paying for that application. I know I'm right because I've seen it over and over again among service contractors seeking to expand technology from the back office into sales, marketing, and customer service. They get sold an "all in one" by their accounting application vendor, and then they are disappointed when it never works well for sales, marketing, and customer service. It's no surprise that accountants make for poor bank bandits.

Still not convinced that focusing on taking money from the customer is the best place to make your technology investments? Do you recall the Amazon story from chapter 2? Jeff Bezos is the best bandit ever when it comes to using technology innovations to take more money from the customer bank. Remember his quotes:

> If there's one reason we have done better than our peers in the Internet space over the last six years, it is because we have focused like a laser on customer experience.

> We see our customers as invited guests to a party, and we are the hosts. It's our job every day to make every important aspect of the customer experience a little bit better.

> The best customer service is if the customer doesn't need to call you, doesn't need to talk to you. It just works.

We've had three big ideas at Amazon that we've stuck with for eighteen years, and they're the reason we're successful: Put the customer first. Invent. And be patient.

These are not the musings of someone who is going to stick up the lemonade stand. Jeff Bezos and Willie Sutton would both ask, "How much money are you going to wring out of the accounting lemonade stand?" "Not much," would be the answer, and then they would direct you back to focusing on taking the money from the folks that have lots of it – in your case it's your prospective customers.

So is 3.5 percent of revenue a high number for technology-application spending? Again, it sort of depends on whether or not you are committed to the How many? How much? and How long? business-value equation presented in chapter 7. If you believe in the economics of growth and a premium brand as the driving factor for shareholder value, it's easy to commit to this level of spending for applications that achieve both growth and pricing power in your market. Jeff Bezos is the wealthiest person on the planet because of his philosophy of focusing technology investment on the customer. If instead of focusing on the customer you are intent on wringing out the maximum amount of cash from the business without any growth in future periods, 3.5 percent of revenue probably makes no sense at all. The only criterion to be considered when growth is not on the agenda is how much administrative expense the application will grind out of the organization.

I will tell you, however, that growing is more fun than grinding. It is also a more scalable way to generate enduring business value. In the next chapter we cover some of the ways that a growth strategy makes running your business easier and more fun than a grind strategy that constantly wrings more money out of the poor neighborhood kids' lemonade stand.

CHAPTER 9

GROWING IS BETTER THAN GRINDING; THE TANGIBLE AND INTANGIBLE BENEFITS OF A GROWTH STRATEGY

People are like dirt. They can either nourish you and help you grow as a person or they can stunt your growth and make you wilt and die.

— Plato

Every Sunday evening I receive an email from the software investment banking team at Key Bank Capital Markets. The subject line of the email is "Software Valuations," and the email contains a link to a weekly report that details the valuation metrics of about 100 different software companies. All of these companies are public corporations, so their stock information is readily available for the folks at Key Bank to analyze. Most of the companies they follow are software as a service (SaaS) companies, and because ServiceTrade is a SaaS company, this report is very interesting to me as the CEO and a shareholder of ServiceTrade. It is my job to maximize the value of our stock for the benefit of all of our shareholders, and the Key Bank team helps me do this through their analysis of SaaS company valuations.

Here is an annotated version of a table they publish for about 70 different SaaS companies. I limited the table to 10 of the entries to make a point about the importance of growth to shareholder value.

	2018	2018	2018
	Growth	Value/Revenue	Price/Earnings
Shopify	51.1%	17.2	NM
ServiceNow	34.4%	12.8	77.1
Carbonite	28.2%	4.4	25
Docusign	26.5%	15.3	NM
Salesforce	25.2%	7.7	57.9
Logmein	22.8%	4.5	20.3
Dropbox	22.6%	9.5	NM
Cision	15.3%	4.6	18.7
Brightcove	7.8%	2.2	NM
ChannelAdvisor	6.8%	2.9	NM

Excerpted from KBCM Technology Group
Software Valuations Report, June 8 Edition

Table 1: Comparison of software as a service company valuations

I sorted these from high to low based on the expected revenue growth rate for 2018. The value-to-revenue multiple indicates how much the total of each company's outstanding stock is worth as a multiple of their anticipated 2018 revenue. The number-one performer is Shopify, with a value-to-revenue multiple of 17.2X. The total value of all outstanding Shopify stock is equal to 17.2 times the revenue expectation for Shopify in 2018. You are reading that correctly. Investors are willing to buy Shopify stock at an extraordinary premium because they believe Shopify is going to grow, grow, grow. And Shopify is delivering on that promise. Note that Shopify expects to grow revenue by 51.1 percent in 2018 compared to their revenue in 2017. That's a terrific growth rate. Also note that Shopify has a value of NM (Not Measured because they are not making a profit) in the category of price-to-earnings. That's because Shopify is going to lose money in 2018. They will probably also lose money in 2019 and 2020 because they are investing like crazy to continue to grow. Despite this lack of profit, their stock is still extremely valuable.

Contrast Shopify with ChannelAdvisor. Their stock trades for just 2.9 times the revenue expectation for 2018. It's interesting that Shopify and ChannelAdvisor offer a similar value proposition with their software applications – they both help small merchants sell their products online. The biggest difference is that Shopify is expected to grow 51.1 percent in 2018 and ChannelAdvisor is expected to grow only 6.8 percent. The expectation of growth explains why Shopify is almost six times more valuable than ChannelAdvisor.

Why is any of this relevant to your business? It is very relevant because their business model is similar to yours in that they sell a subscription program to their customers. If you are following my advice and developing a subscription program for maintenance, monitoring, and inspections for which you sell an annual or longer contract, your business is similar to these companies, and investors will ultimately value your business in the same way they value these businesses. The point I am trying to make is that growing is better than grinding when it comes to creating value for shareholders.

Grinding means pushing everyone in the organization to squeeze more profit from the current revenue stream. I have nothing against profit, and I think you should aim to be profitable.

But grinding does not significantly increase the value of your business if there is the possibility to *grow* the business instead.

Growing is much more fun for everyone than grinding, for all of the obvious reasons. Growing means that new stuff is happening all the time. New products are being introduced to the market. New customers are being served. New employees are joining the company to help take care of the new customers. New promotions are being handed out because there is more responsibility to be shared. New offices are being opened. New equipment is being purchased. New tools are being deployed. New training is underway on how to use new tools. New, new, new means fun, fun, fun.

Grinding sucks because old tools are breaking and not being replaced. Old employees are leaving and not being replaced, or taking on more responsibility for no increase in pay. Old customers are complaining because they are not getting good service. Old trucks are breaking down and disrupting the workday. Old, old, old means suck, suck, suck.

What is your plan for growth? How are you going to orient your company in a direction that gets to the fun of growing? It begins with a commitment to growth. If there is no expectation in the company that growth is an important metric, then no growth will occur. Set growth targets as part of your planning process, and don't be shy about asking people to stretch to achieve something ambitious. For organic growth, plan to grow by 15 percent per year, and think about pushing for 20 to 30 percent (depending on the size of your company). All the best employees in your business will rally around the growth goal because none of them signed on for a career in which not much is achieved. Your employees will get much more career development from an aggressive growth strategy.

Here are some ideas that can be part of your plan for growth:

Hire more salespeople. One of the easiest ways to grow is to invest more money in the sales function. Because salespeople generally earn most of their income from commissions, they are highly motivated to sign new customers. If you have a great digital wrap and a terrific subscription program, they have something cool to demonstrate and review with customers. The new accounts the sales team signs will stay with you forever once they experience the value of your subscription program, and you can invest in more salespeople yet again because you are confident in your future cash flow.

Start an apprenticeship program. If you add new customers you will need to add new technicians. No doubt they are difficult to find, so start an apprenticeship program in which you bring in raw talent straight out of high school or through vocational programs in your area. There are often nice tax incentives if you create and register the program with your state department of labor. The pressure of getting new apprentices busy with quality work leads everyone in the organization to have a sales-oriented mentality.

Add a new product or service. Innovation is fun, and your customers will happily give you more money for new program services that allow them to consolidate vendors or use less contracted labor in exchange for technology-enabled equipment monitoring, as an example. Developing a couple of mini startup enterprises focused on delivering a new innovation to the market keeps everyone excited about a new and highly scalable revenue stream. Not all of them will be successes, so make certain everyone knows that the important outcome is a quality process that takes risks, involves the customer, and stretches the boundaries of your company's technical expertise. Some of these projects will likely be big hits that energize the organization and lead to substantial new revenue.

Buy a complementary company. There are companies in adjacent geographical markets delivering services similar to yours, and there are companies in your market that carry trade licenses for services that you do not currently offer. Spend time networking with these folks because there is no threat to sharing ideas and ambitions with them. If you have an amazing digital wrap and a highly successful subscription program, they may want to join up with you to expand the market you serve. I don't generally recommend attempting to buy direct competitors because it is an awkward dance unless they approach you – and then it is still awkward. Similar to an affair with a neighbor's spouse, it is difficult to imagine how everyone emerges happy on the other side of a competitive acquisition.

Quote more repairs. If you don't already have a dedicated sales team for selling repairs and upgrades to existing customers, maybe now is the time to make that change. I like separating repair sales from new-client prospecting because it's a different type of work that is better suited to a different type of salesperson. Quoting repairs is like farming, while new-client prospecting is more like hunting. Let the farmers farm and the hunters hunt. Repair sales require the technical skills to review deficiencies reported by the technicians and quickly turn them into quotes for the customer to review and approve; new-client prospecting is more about tracking down potential customers based on the trail they leave in the market – different skills for different work. Form a repair sales team and get the technicians involved so they know how to report deficiencies in a way that sets up the repair sale more easily. Pictures, videos, and technical insights from the customer location give the repair salesperson a great boost in getting the customer over the line for each repair recommendation. There is no better lead in the world than an existing problem that your company is qualified to repair. And be sure the customer can just click the button above those pictures and videos to accept the quote.

Request more reviews. Growth is often gated by a lack of interested prospects. People are busy, and cold-calling often feels like you're interrupting instead of offering to solve a problem. However, some prospects in your market already have a problem that you can solve because they are ready to fire their current vendor. Be certain that they find you when they decide their old vendor has got to go. The best way to maximize your presence on the Internet is through a robust online review program. ServiceTrade includes a review program that allows technicians to request the review as part of the final customer sign-off, with zero extra administrative burden as the core principle of the digital wrap strategy dictates. When a prospect decides that their current vendor is not getting the job done, your company will be easy to find online, and the 1,000 or more positive reviews you have will make you seem like the obvious choice. When they call, the salesperson engages with a prospect who is ready to make a change and is all warmed up by the quality of your online reputation.

Maximizing the value of your business is the most tangible outcome associated with a successful growth strategy. The difference in valuation of the companies tracked by Key Bank in the SaaS market based on their respective growth rates is extravagant, and it should be a lesson for anyone who wants to build value with a subscription business model. The intangible value of having a growth strategy is that you will attract, develop, and retain a better class of employees who value your company because they expect to experience greater career development. They will be exposed to ever-increasing levels of responsibility, which leads to higher job satisfaction and better retention. Growing is fun and grinding sucks, so aim for growth and get more pay and have more fun along the way.

In the next two chapters we go into further detail regarding two of the critical elements of a growth strategy: recruiting a new generation of employees and delivering on technical innovations that allow you to charge customers more money. In chapter 10 we explore how to find and motivate the millennial-generation employee prospects who represent your new employment pool using digital wrap tricks to gain their attention. In chapter 11 we cover some of the technological trends that dominate much of the trade press, and attempt to separate the bluster and the hype from the practical steps you can take to begin to add these innovations to your customer program offerings.

CHAPTER 10

SHAWN SAYS, "EASY TO FIND, EASY TO HIRE"; USING YOUR DIGITAL WRAP TO WIN THE BATTLE FOR TALENT.

Youth loves honor and victory more than money.
—Aristotle

In a late 2017 visit with a customer, I was startled to hear the owner and president of the company declare, "It's time to start pulling back because the economy is about to tank." I gave him a funny look because the economy was booming, with unemployment below 4 percent and new construction going gangbusters. "What makes you believe the economy is about to tank?" I respectfully asked. He replied, "We have gotten over forty job inquiries from technicians who work for our competitors in just the last three weeks. Whenever we get that kind of inbound interest for work, it means that a recession is about to hit."

It didn't make any sense. I thought about it some more, and then I asked, "Didn't you guys start doing online reviews with ServiceTrade about six months ago?" He replied, "We did." I asked further, "And haven't you already collected over six hundred reviews on your website?" He replied, "We have." I sat back and grinned. "Your digital wrap is driving inbound interest for employment at your company. You guys completely redesigned your website for search engine optimization and adopted the customer review platform. It takes a little time, but now that's not only paying off in new customers, but also in prospective employees."

Your truck wrap has always been a recruiting tool. Just by performing their day-to-day work and driving around town, your technicians and the trucks they drive market your brand to potential customers and employees. A Mercedes Sprinter with a well-designed wrap is going to leave a good impression. A beat-up 15-year-old Ford Econoline with a few decals designed in the nineties... not so much. But you already knew that.

What most service companies don't realize is that a digital wrap works the same way. Just by performing the day-to-day work and generating online content for your customers, your technicians market your brand to potential employees as well. A well-designed website that shows up at the top of Google search results thanks to hundreds of great reviews collected by technicians leaves a good impression. A 16-year-old website that looks like it was designed before the dot-com bust... not so much.

Modern workers look online to evaluate potential employers. If your company is not easy to find on Google, strike one. If there are no online reviews or all of the reviews are bad, strike two. If your website is an incoherent word salad without compelling imagery and video case studies, strike three – you're out of consideration. If you have a great digital wrap, however, job applicants will come to you. Hiring is easier because people want to work for a premium brand they can trust.

If you're going to grow, you need to hire technicians to fuel that growth. If you're going to hire skilled labor, you'd better be thinking about your online presence and reputation because that is the combat zone you must navigate today to impress new recruits. Your digital wrap strategy is a critical element of your growth strategy because it helps you attract both new customers and new employees.

Recruiting new employees is not much different from selling to new customers. A recruiting pipeline is similar to a sales pipeline in that you must identify prospects, work the prospects to convert them into employees, and then hang on to them for the long haul through a great work experience. With this sales pipeline metaphor as a guide, let's review each stage of the employee hiring process and some insights and advice about how you might generate a bounty of talent as our customer in the story above did.

Find More Prospects

The first step in a recruiting pipeline is identical to that of a sales pipeline: find more prospects to keep your pool of opportunity fresh and full. Finding more prospects is easier if they are finding you first because of your outstanding reputation. An April 2017 poll by Glassdoor and Harris found that 84 percent of job-seekers indicated that the reputation of a company is important as they consider their choices for a new employer. (https://www.thelasallenetwork.com/wp-content/uploads/2018/02/65-hr-and-recruiting-stats-for-2018-min.pdf)

Reputation has always been important when recruiting talent because the best techs want to work at the best companies. However, the medium through which your reputation spreads has changed. Word of mouth is still important, but it pales in comparison to your company's online reputation, or lack thereof. Before a job-seeker even applies, your website, social media presence, and online reviews help them through the first two phases of the job hunt: discovery and research. If they don't already know about your company brand, your website and reviews should drive discovery because your brand is easy to find online through search engine optimization. Once they discover your brand, your online reputation should drive their research to the conclusion that you are a great company to work for and that they should apply.

When a technician starts their job hunt, they use Google to search for companies in their industry, and the top results are the first companies they research. The top search results are the best bet, and searching for local companies is no exception. Fortunately the fresh, dynamic content created by your digital wrap is exactly the kind of indicator Google uses to rank websites in search results. Just by performing the day-to-day tasks associated with the services you offer, your techs are collecting customer reviews and generating rich content that helps prospective employees discover your company.

Millennials represent your most important new employee pool, and they almost exclusively find and research new job opportunities online. Most of my millennial friends discovered, researched, and applied for their current job completely online without talking to a single person. From discovery on Google or a job board to exhaustive research of prospective companies, they did everything on their laptop or smartphone. They browsed the company website and social media for information about the mission and culture. Where applicable, they researched customer reviews. They paid especially close attention to the reviews from current and past employees.

Ninety-two percent of working Americans consider employer reviews to be important when deciding to apply for a job.
— iCIMS, The Modern Job Seeker Report 2017
*(https://cdn31.icims.com/drupal/icims2_files/prod/s3fs-public/hei_*
assets/Modern-Job-Seeker-Report%20Final.pdf)

Indeed and Glassdoor, two of the largest job-listing websites, are the dominant players when it comes to company reviews by former and current employees. When you search online for a company by name, the employee ratings of that company on Indeed and Glassdoor are often in the top results. A potential employee can very quickly see what actual employees think about a company. This can work in your favor or it can be a strike against you.

From a job-seeker's perspective, zero employee reviews is concerning, a bunch of bad reviews is a death knell, and a mix of mostly good reviews is a great sign. I say a mix because people are suspicious when all reviews are five-star ones. As with customer reviews, it's acceptable to ask your employees to leave a review of your company; just be sure that the review truly represents what *they* think, not what *you* think. Do not instruct them to leave a good review. Should you get a negative review, be responsive and respectful. Don't punish someone who posts a bad review. If you do not already have a healthy presence on Indeed and Glassdoor, encourage employees to rate your company on these sites. Online reviews of any type – customer or employee – are a key element of a snazzy digital wrap.

Top five pieces of information job seekers want employers to provide as they research where to work: 1) Salary/compensation, 2) Benefits, 3) Basic company information, 4) What makes it an attractive place to work, 5) Company mission, vision, values. (Glassdoor U.S. Site Survey, January 2016)
— Glassdoor "Top HR Statistics"
(https://www.glassdoor.com/employers/popular-topics/hr-stats.htm)

When employee prospects find your website online, before they apply they are going to assess:

- What does the company stand for?
- What's it like to work for the company?
- Are the company values evident in daily operations?
- Does the culture fit my values?
- Is the work environment fun and challenging?
- Will I be able to grow, learn new skills, and advance?

If they like what they see, they will be motivated to contact you. You should provide a simple, online application process with minimal barriers for the applicant to send you their information. A simple, mobile-friendly web form that solicits their name, phone number, and email from a call-to-action like "Are you a skilled technician and want to learn more about working at Aardvark Services?" garners a lot more responses than a byzantine application process that asks candidates every possible question and requires them to upload a resume. You'll definitely do more work to qualify candidates, but in the midst of a skilled labor shortage that's an acceptable cost. Keep it simple. If you don't already have an online mechanism to collect prospective employee information and promote open positions, update your website as soon as possible – like tomorrow.

Even when you have no openings you should always be recruiting on your website. List the most in-demand jobs permanently. Just as with prospective customers, you always have the choice to upgrade your portfolio by eliminating troublemakers and finding more attractive new prospects.

59% [of job seekers] used social media to research the company culture of organizations they were interested in.
—Jobvite, Job Seeker National Survey, 2016
*(https://www.jobvite.com/wp-content/uploads/2016/03/Jobvite_*
Jobseeker_Nation_2016.pdf)

Social media is also a powerful tool when recruiting, especially Facebook and LinkedIn. Job-seekers review a company's social media profile and posts to learn about the brand. They expect to find a more relaxed representation of the company's environment on social media sites than on the corporate website. Posts about company events, employees, and corporate values go a long way to help job-seekers get a better feel for the company. The Jobvite survey cited above found that 51 percent of workers were satisfied but open to a new job.

It would be nice if you could meet all your hiring demand with a flood of great candidates who found you online. That is unlikely, so you also need an active recruiting strategy to fill your prospect pipeline. One way to find digitally savvy candidates is by searching LinkedIn for your competitors' employees. Send them InMail introducing yourself and your company. If that doesn't work, use a product like Hunter.io to find their work email address, and email them directly. For example, if Hunter.io tells you that the email address format for the company is [first].[last]@[company].com and you are trying to reach Marty McFly at Aardvark Service, his email address is probably marty.mcfly@aardvarkservice.net.

For entry-level office and field positions, one ServiceTrade customer, Guardian Fire Protection, has another interesting recruiting approach. Once a month they host an open-door interview day. Anyone who shows up is guaranteed an interview. Some interviews are much shorter than others, but everyone gets a shot. They advertise the event through Craigslist, social media, and their own website. For a relatively low investment of time and money, they've filled multiple open positions. When they ask successful candidates who show up on the interview day why they didn't just apply online, candidates often say that they didn't feel like their resume was good enough.

Hire More Employees

After you have identified a nice pool of candidates, you face the task of converting the best ones into actual employees. Many contractors struggle to bring young people into their companies, but understanding what's important to millennials in their job hunt is the first step toward creating a more attractive career offering for them. A 2014 *Harvard Business Review* article showed in a bar chart that nearly 80 percent of millennials looked for people and culture fit with employers, followed by career potential. (https://hbr.org/2014/03/how-companies-can-attract-the-best-college-talent)

Have you ever had a candidate ask you what it's like to work at your company? I have. Like a lot of hiring managers I had trouble explaining exactly what the ServiceTrade culture is like; the same was true for our entire executive team. To solve the riddle of describing our culture, we assembled a group of non-executive employees to come up with a clear description of the ServiceTrade culture. One person from each of the teams — development, marketing, support, and sales — gathered feedback from teammates about their experiences working at ServiceTrade. All of that feedback was aggregated and discussed by a newly formed culture committee. A couple of interesting themes emerged. First, ServiceTrade employees are inquisitive and curious, and they are empowered to explore their professional interests as part of their work routine. Second, ServiceTrade employees are bold and constructively challenge coworkers, managers, and customers. Employees are encouraged to voice their professional opinions.

Understanding these core tenets simplified our hiring process. During the interview process, it's easy to spot a candidate who fits the culture because they tend to ask a lot of great questions and they are willing to challenge assumptions. Obviously these aren't the only traits we look for, but they're a great indicator of how successful someone will be at ServiceTrade. On the other side of the table, candidates tend to be very attracted to our company culture if they think the culture is a good fit for them when we describe it or let them experience it during the interview process.

If you cannot quickly describe your work environment and how it is unique to your company, it's probably worth the effort to go through an exercise similar to the one undertaken at ServiceTrade. If you don't like what you discover, consider changes you might make to modify the outcome over the long term. In any case, providing a few short sentences that describe the culture of the work environment helps you close the deal or avoid a recruiting mismatch when you make a job offer.

Keep Great Employees Longer

Similar to holding on to customers for as long as possible and consistently finding ways to get more revenue from them (remember the "How long?" question from chapter 7?), holding on to good employees is the final and most rewarding element of a successful recruiting pipeline. After investing in training and acclimating them to your culture and the unique value you provide for customers, you want them to make their contributions to those positive outcomes for as long a period as possible.

64% of Millennials would rather make $40K a year at a job they love, than $100K a year at a job they think is boring. (The Columbus Dispatch, Study Conducted by the Intelligence Group, 2014)
— Glassdoor "Top HR Statistics"
(https://www.glassdoor.com/employers/popular-topics/hr-stats.htm)

Not all millennials are the same, but data suggests that they have very different career priorities than those of other generations. They typically prioritize career happiness above financial gain. Happiness at work is derived from career progression, satisfying work, having an impact, and working with people they like. Projecting a safe 20-year path with a conservative retirement plan will not help you retain most millennial employees. Fun, interesting, and impactful work will do more to hold them at your company than any promise of long-term financial rewards.

60% of Millennials consider the most attractive perk to be growth opportunities. (Glassdoor survey, March 2013)
—Glassdoor "Top HR Statistics"
(https://www.glassdoor.com/employers/popular-topics/hr-stats.htm)

One idea for retaining millennials is to offer them more challenging work. If they value career progression and making an impact, prioritize a work program that gets them more involved in solving the challenges of the business. Let them point your company toward innovations and operating capabilities that have big positive impacts on the value of your company to your customers. Yes, I said, "have them point your company" and not the other way around. Let me explain what I mean.

Senior managers are typically well equipped for understanding the challenges of the business and its strategic direction, but generally ill-suited for actually solving problems. They see the impact of problems in the results, but are not close enough to the work to solve the problems. Why not have the employees do it? Consider defining a set of high-level challenges that are consistent themes for competitiveness in your business. Here are some potential examples:

- A higher ratio of maintenance revenue to emergency-call revenue every quarter
- Double-digit annual growth
- Double-digit technician revenue productivity every year
- One new technician hire every month
- One new service-product introduction every year
- One new data-collection productivity breakthrough every year

If your employees have a good handle on the strategic rocks they need to turn over, they will often hand you the solutions and the results you are seeking while simultaneously tying themselves closer to your business because they feel the impact they are making. An example from ServiceTrade is our online training curriculum. One of our strategic goals is to reduce the amount of effort and expense required to onboard new customers. It is part of our growth strategy. If every customer requires lots of our consultants' time to learn the application and become productive, it's either expensive for us or expensive for them. We turned that problem over to David Varnedoe, one of our senior customer-success consultants, because he indicated a real interest in scalable training technology.

David selected the platform we now use to deliver the training and developed all the content for the courses. It has been such a success that now David works full time only on online training products. He owns it internally, but the benefit of the platform is felt across almost all functions in the organization. It's a great example because David made an impact through work that he is passionate to deliver, and the training program drives us toward a strategic outcome: less expense for successful customer application adoption.

If you consider your employee recruitment as another sales pipeline, your digital wrap will help you attract the best staff in a tight labor market. Just as with sales prospects and customers, make it easy for job-seekers and current employees to find and engage with your company online. Lower the barriers for them to see and understand your unique value and culture (remember the "Who do you think you are?" exercises from chapter 4?). Just like better hand tools and nicer trucks have always helped recruiting, so do a better digital wrap and a work culture that values employee innovations. Lowering expenses for hiring and keeping great employees is one more way that a digital wrap delivers money for nothing.

CHAPTER 11

AI, IoT, BIG DATA, AND THE ALPHABET SOUP OF TECHNOLOGY JARGON YOU NEED TO UNDERSTAND

Our business is infested with idiots who try to impress by using pretentious jargon.
— *David Ogilvy, founder of Ogilvy and Mather*

In 1984 I was 17 years old and working as an usher in a movie theater when the science fiction thriller *The Terminator* was released. It was a surprise hit, and I must have seen the movie a couple dozen times between actually screening it (I got to go to movies for free as a theater employee) and sneaking into the theater to watch after the concession stand closed. In case you are not familiar with the movie, Arnold Schwarzenegger plays a human-like cyborg – a Terminator – sent from the future with a mission to kill Sarah Connor, the mother of the future resistance leader who is fighting the Terminator's artificial intelligence master, Skynet.

Aside from the obvious standout qualities of Schwarzenegger's physique (a former Mr. Universe and Mr. Olympia) and the incredible strength demonstrated by the cyborg, the Terminator looks and even acts somewhat human. To remind the audience that the Terminator is actually a very sophisticated computer, director James Cameron sometimes displays the action from the perspective of the Terminator.

In these "look through" scenes the audience is presented with a screen that is apparently the field of vision of the Terminator. The film color quality is replaced with mostly red, white, and black imagery. Superimposed on the imagery is a bunch of scrolling gibberish and some highlighted, flashing boxes to call attention to certain data elements the Terminator is analyzing – a person's body size, weapons in the hands of potential antagonists that must be foiled, etc. Of course, if the Terminator was really a sophisticated computer cyborg, there would not be an internal display barfing computer gibberish onto a screen in a manner readable by humans. Computers do not need to read data in order to respond to it. The Terminator would simply ingest external data via his camera eyes and his microphone ears and other sensors that detect temperature, pressure, odor, and what not. He would then make judgments and take actions that would accomplish the mission: the termination of Sarah Connor. All of this would happen without a screen display.

Why am I talking about *The Terminator*? Why is the detail of the Terminator's view of the world as depicted by the movie director important? Because it illustrates that artificial intelligence (AI), the Internet of things (IoT), big data, and all the rest of the alphabet soup puked up on a daily basis by technology media and vendors hyping their products is generally nothing more than the collective, gradual evolution of computers – they are already part of the arsenal of technology you are using for the benefit of your customer. In 1984 James Cameron could imagine a computer that understood and spoke natural language, saw real-time imagery, reacted to its environment, and took actions to accomplish a mission. To portray the Terminator as a sophisticated AI being, Cameron showed the audience what computers looked like to the masses in 1984 – a somewhat low-resolution screen with scrolling, digitized text and an occasional option that would become highlighted when the cyborg selected it. (Remember, the mouse was a new thing in 1984; the first Apple Macintosh computers shipped that year.) Cameron could not assume that the audience would make the leap to his futuristic interpretation of an AI-enabled cyborg, so he showed the audience a 1984 computer interface to make certain they got the connection. All this stuff in the media about AI, IoT, machine learning, big data, blah, blah, blah is just the real world catching up to what James Cameron predicted would happen way back in 1984.

Today we are talking to our phone to have it dial our best friend. We are issuing verbal commands to our Alexa assistant to have it order pizza or play a favorite radio station. Our Nest thermostat is monitoring our habits, such as when we come and go, along with our preferences for ambient temperature, in order to take actions regarding raising and lowering the temperature where we live. These common applications of AI would have been totally foreign and inconceivable to a movie audience in 1984. But James Cameron had a vision of what artificial intelligence could potentially accomplish in the future, and he did a really good job of presenting that vision to the audience in a way that they could understand. Part of my goal with this chapter is to wave away the mystique of technology and replace it with simple and practical realities. Let's do a quick reset on some of the favorite overhyped terms from the technology media – AI, IoT, and big data.

Artificial intelligence: AI is just the trend toward computers ingesting more diverse data in more formats (such as images, audio, natural language, pressure, temperature, humidity, etc.) to enable analysis that leads to judgments and actions related to accomplishing a mission or objective. Because AI is more of a trend than a definitive end state, AI can be simply classified as Hofstadter, a famous AI scientist, described it: "AI is whatever hasn't been done yet." More accurately, AI is simply the leading edge of new capability for computers to operate more intelligently on a broader diversity of data.

Internet of things: IoT is simply the trend of more and more things being connected to the Internet in order to send or receive data or act on data received. Connections to the Internet have historically been through people staring at screens – and increasingly listening to audio speakers – and entering data or responding to data received. "Things," whether a cyborg like the Terminator or a $10 temperature sensor, don't need screens (or keyboards or a mouse or speakers) to send and receive data or act on data received.

Big data: Big data is simply the collection and analysis of data sets that are too large for humans to effectively parse, analyze, and extract intelligence from using simple programs like Excel. Ever-cheaper storage and computing cycles have led to ever-increasing data collection, storage, and analysis. Again, big data is simply a trend and not a definitive end state.

It is tempting to believe that all critical innovations in the future will fit into categories similar to AI, IoT, and big data. I have a story from MIT, however, that I want to use to refute this notion. In sharp contrast to Cameron's 1984 vision of artificial intelligence, it's a classroom experience from 1994 – 10 years after *The Terminator:*

Alexander Slocum was the most entertaining and passionate professor I encountered during my time at MIT. He taught a graduate course in the school of mechanical engineering called Design of Precision Machines. The course was meant to educate a new generation of engineers in the principles that might help them design the next silicon wafer-stepper – a highly precise machine used in the manufacture of integrated circuits – or the next high-speed precision surface-grinder. It has been over 24 years since I was in his classroom, but I still remember one of the lessons he conveyed in typical sarcastic and practical terms.

Professor Slocum was a big fan of using software and computers to solve problems, but he was also a great engineer, meaning that he was always seeking the most practical and elegant approach to solving a problem. He was describing to the class how a software application might be used to model tool deflection errors and to use a polynomial algorithm based on a hysteresis model to eliminate errors in precision machining. He indicated that one of his graduate students had spent better than 2,000 hours on the programming model and generated nearly a million lines of code. Then he dryly informed us, "The better way to solve this problem is to invest in a ten-thousand-pound slab of granite from New Hampshire to encase the grinding platform and eliminate all the errors. Never use computers to solve a problem that can be better handled with a ten-thousand-pound rock."

I cracked up. Obviously the lesson stuck with me if I can still remember his words 24 years later. I bring up the wisdom of Professor Slocum, who is a nerd's nerd at an elite technical institution, to make a point about innovation. Technology is important, but always be practical. Ten years after *The Terminator* showed us the possibility of technology doing human-like things better than humans, a top scientist at a top technical institute was recommending a 10,000-pound rock as a solution that was superior to a million lines of computer code. I will say again that technology is important, but always be practical.

Over time computers will progress to read a broader spectrum of inputs, make more sophisticated judgments, and take an increasing variety of actions that lead to desired outcomes. No one was talking about AI in 1984 – no one in the mainstream media anyway, because the topic was confined to a small group of computer nerds at top technical institutions like Stanford and MIT. Yet the director of *The Terminator* could imagine a future in which a computer becomes so powerful it can measure its environment in a human-like manner, make judgments based on those measurements, and take intelligent actions to execute a mission, in that case the termination of Sarah Connor. It is unlikely that anyone who saw *The Terminator* in 1984 remembers the on-screen effects Cameron used to connect the audience to the idea that the Terminator was a computer. I bet everyone who saw the movie remembers the Terminator's mission, however. What was the mission? To terminate Sarah Connor, of course.

Whether an innovation can correctly be labeled as AI (or as any other overhyped term of the day) is far less important than whether the innovation helps accomplish the mission. The Terminator's mission was to terminate Sarah Connor, and the Terminator was extremely well suited for carrying out the mission (although it actually failed). Defining the mission that you would like to accomplish with AI, IoT, big data, etc. is much more important, in my humble opinion, than the technology you select to achieve the mission. It may be that a 10,000-pound slab of granite is the best technology for the mission, or maybe not. Have you thought about the mission you want to accomplish using technology?

What you likely want to accomplish through technology is to maximize customer equipment performance while eliminating equipment failures so that your customer experiences the least risk, expense, and disruption in their business. The reason technology is important as an enabler of this mission is that it is generally cheaper and easier to manage than people. If you accomplish this mission, your customer will spend zero dollars recovering from disruptions (lost output, spoiled inventory, damaged property, emergency services) while maximizing the amount of money they spend with you relative to other suppliers.

Let's rearrange the alphabet soup of technology jargon to come up with a simple question – a technology strategy test – that helps you cut through the hype and delivers some focus for your technology strategy. I'm going to drop a few words from artificial intelligence, Internet of things, and big data to make my point. Here we go:

How can you use the **Internet** to collect **data** about customer equipment so that you and your customer can make **intelligent** decisions about services that will minimize risk, expense, and business disruptions caused by suboptimal equipment performance or equipment failure?

I really don't care whether the data is "big" or "small." I don't care whether the information that comes over the Internet is generated by a "thing" or by a person holding a smartphone taking photos of an impaired piece of equipment. I also don't care if the "intelligence" is artificial or natural, so long as it is smart and not dumb. The overall direction of technology as computing gets cheaper and people get more expensive is toward bigger data, more things connected to the Internet, and more intelligence that is artificial versus natural. None of these trends mean, however, that every technological solution is better than a 10,000-pound slab of granite.

Now that we have generated a simple question that cuts through the hype and focuses our innovation lens on practical and actionable solutions, what are some examples that illustrate the potential value of this strategy? How are you currently and in the future going to collect data over the Internet to make more intelligent decisions regarding equipment services that should be delivered to optimize performance? You don't have to wait for the day that the Terminator is a reality. Technology evolves continuously, and you simply need to commit yourself to being in the stream of innovation for the benefit of your customer.

The favorite workflow of ServiceTrade customers is for the technician to record equipment deficiencies using a mobile app, which prompts the salesperson to generate a quote for the service needed, which the customer then reviews and hopefully approves. Let's see if this workflow meets our technology strategy test. Are we collecting information about equipment via the Internet? Yes. In this case it is photo, video, audio, and text captured by the technician that illustrate the problem to the salesperson in the office and ultimately to the customer. Are we using intelligence? Yes. The technician knows this situation can lead to a failure, otherwise why record it? The salesperson also recognizes the problem because of the detailed data set, and applies the correct quote template for repair based on prior experience – how much time, which tools, which parts, etc. Finally, the customer can make a good decision because they see and hear the problem and can trust the information. Just like the "look through" scenes in *The Terminator*, the customer sees what the technician sees.

Here is another example: Sensors are getting super cheap, and the power requirements are getting so small that battery life is often measured in years (check out Monnit online). Consider sprinkler customers who have pipes at risk of bursting due to freezing in areas of their facilities that are not temperature controlled. A temperature sensor that generates a freeze alert when the temperature drops to 32 degrees can trigger a response to turn on some space heaters. If the heaters are connected to a "smart" electrical circuit, they can deploy on the signal without any intervention. (This seems like a no-brainer, but during cold snaps in normally moderate climates, it is amazing how many sprinkler pipes freeze.) Does it pass the test? Did we collect data on the Internet? Yes – through an ad hoc temperature sensor. Are we using intelligence? Yes. Intelligent people know that water freezes at 32 degrees, and we know that turning on a space heater keeps the temperature above that threshold. Did our decision and action avoid disruption and maintain optimal facility performance? Yes. Great, we are off to a terrific start with our AI, IoT, and big data strategy!

Now let's get big data involved. Big data is simply a buzzterm for datasets that are so large that a simple tool like Excel with a human interface might struggle to parse any intelligence from the data. A good example is the sum of all information and data collected about a customer in their ServiceTrade account. No one could read or parse that much information with a simple tool. However, all the data in ServiceTrade is automatically ported over to Amazon's Redshift/QuickSight big-data analytics platform. A simple analysis in QuickSight can show a customer's spending habits related to emergency service versus planned services (preventative maintenance and planned retrofits and repairs). During an annual review with a challenging customer who insists on minimal preventative maintenance, you might be able to demonstrate that a similar customer who opted for maximum preventative maintenance has spent significantly less overall during the course of the past three years.

No one could parse that amount of data in Excel, but QuickSight handles it easily with just a few clicks. Does it pass the test? Did we collect data on the Internet? Yes. All data in ServiceTrade is collected over the Internet because ServiceTrade is a SaaS application. Did we make an intelligent decision to lower expenses, lower risk, and optimize performance? Hopefully the answer is yes, because ideally the customer buys into your premium program based on the analysis that indicates lower total costs.

Let's quickly contrast these straightforward examples of effective and simple technology deployment for achieving a well-defined mission with a "technology solution trying to find a problem." Google, Snapchat, Intel, and a host of other technology heavyweights have spent years and hundreds of millions of dollars on "smart glasses" that combine cameras, heads-up displays, natural language recognition, cellular networking, etc. Some vendors in the contracting space latched on to this science experiment and began selling it as the productivity solution for all of your problems. According to these vendors it enabled customer collaboration, technician training, remote diagnosis, and a host of other benefits. It didn't work.

Taken in pieces, elements of the technology make sense. A small Bluetooth camera clipped to the bill of a ball cap with a similar Bluetooth earpiece, all tethered to a mobile phone, enables the technician to fire up a FaceTime, Slack, or Skype call with a colleague. The two can then collaborate via shared images and real-time conversation to diagnose a problem. But jamming everything into glasses is a laboratory exercise instead of a solution to a problem. It is Frankenstein's monster compared to the Terminator. Frankenstein's invention was great science, but yielded only chaos and misery when deployed beyond the lab. The Terminator, by contrast, was built for accomplishing the mission in the field.

Your objective is to assemble the Terminator and avoid Frankenstein's monster. The examples above clearly indicate that AI, IoT, and big data are already part of the arsenal of technology you are using for the benefit of your customer. It really is not rocket science, and you really can embrace new innovations if you are willing to explore and set aside the intimidating jargon in favor of an elegant strategy. Your strategy should simply be collecting more data via the Internet so you can intelligently make service decisions that optimize the performance of your customers' important equipment. Any innovation that meets this simple test is putting you on a good path for adding more value. The solution can be a 10,000-pound slab of granite or a human-like cyborg capable of carrying out an extraordinarily complex and dangerous mission. Stay focused on the mission, and the right solutions will present themselves as obvious candidates for your premium service program.

CHAPTER 12

A BRAND IN THE HAND IS THE FUTURE OF PREMIUM CUSTOMER SERVICE; GETTING READY TO RUN A MOBILE MARATHON

If you want to run, run a mile.
If you want to experience a different life, run a marathon.
— Emil Zatopek, Olympian and gold medalist

Apple is the most valuable company in the world with a market capitalization exceeding $1 trillion. Approximately 75 percent of Apple's annual revenue of about $250 billion comes from the iPhone and services consumed from the iPhone (music, apps, movies, etc.). Another technology behemoth, Facebook, was founded just 14 years ago and already its annual revenue is approaching $50 billion per year. Ninety percent of Facebook's 2018 revenue comes from mobile advertisements, and they just began mobile advertising in 2012! Mobile riches are not just for technology companies either. Anyone following ServiceTrade's blog knows that we write again and again about Domino's and the breakout success they have enjoyed because of mobile technology for customer engagement. And they are not alone.

Chick-fil-A has ranked number one for the past three years for customer satisfaction in the fast-food category, according to the American Customer Satisfaction Index's annual surveys. (https://www.qsrmagazine.com/fast-food/study-chick-fil-has-most-satisfied-customers) I fully expect Chick-fil-A to continue to dominate in customer service because they have what I believe is the best mobile app in the fast-food space. Chick-fil-A One is what they call their mobile app, and I can shop from their menu (with pictures of every item, of course) and send my order to a nearby store. The app knows my location, so when I arrive at the store they begin preparing my order. I never have to wait in line, and I also earn free food for being a frequent user of the mobile app. Starbucks is also a big winner in the mobile customer service space. They were the first to market with a mobile app to help relieve congestion in the stores and make it more convenient to visit Starbucks. You may know how good the apps make you feel as a customer of these outlets, but you probably don't know the business impact of being the market leader for customer service in your category. It is good.

Chick-fil-A restaurants averaged $4.4 million annual sales per store in 2016, according to a survey released by QSR Magazine. (https://www.qsrmagazine.com/content/qsr50-2017-top-50-chart) The next highest quick-service restaurant is Whataburger at $2.7 million in annual sales per store. And Chick-fil-A isn't even open on Sunday! – they are achieving these results with 14 percent less capacity than other restaurants. You're probably thinking to yourself that the 2016 results have nothing to do with Chick-fil-A's mobile success, and you're correct. But that is exactly the point that I want to make. Chick-fil-A was already the leader in customer service and revenue *before* they launched their mobile experience. They were not content with their success. They made a big investment to lead in the mobile space, and I wager their results will reflect the positive impact of that leadership. I am confident of Chick-fil-A's success because the success at Starbucks has already been measured.

Starbucks launched their mobile app in early 2011, and it included a mobile pay feature similar to a gift card. They beat Apple and Samsung, technology giants, to the mobile pay party. Imagine that – a coffee store scooping companies like Apple and Samsung! Mobile innovation has paid off for Starbucks; they reported that in the third quarter of 2017 approximately 30 percent of sales were transacted using the mobile app. The real win, however, is that mobile app users are spending three times more than other customers! This might be a chicken-and-egg situation in which the most frequent Starbucks customers get the most value from the app so they are naturally the biggest spenders, but who cares? Starbucks delivered an innovation that helps assure the loyalty of their best customers. They are maximizing the How much? and How long? measurements discussed in chapter 7.

All these stories of mobile riches make perfect sense if you just take a look around you anytime you're out in public. Fifty percent of the folks you see have their noses in their phones, and the other 50 percent all have their phones within arm's reach. These devices measure our workouts and even our sleep quality. The phone has bridged not only the last mile to the customer but literally the last three feet. If your brand is mobile, you are always within arm's reach of serving the customer.

If you are committed to leading in your market – if you expect to be the premium brand that is known for outstanding customer service – you must be committed to leading in mobile customer service just like Chick-fil-A and Starbucks. Fortunately it doesn't have to happen overnight, and there is still plenty of whitespace in the market. No one owns this space or has such a lead that you are forced to follow their example. You can define your mobile future.

I believe the race to mobile customer service in service contracting is going to be a marathon and not a sprint. Just like a marathon, competitiveness begins with a commitment to a training routine. Using the marathon metaphor, let's lay out a basic program to get you prepared to compete for mobile dominance in your market.

Basic Fitness

No one serious about marathon competition just wakes up one day and decides to run a race the following day or even the following week or month. A basic level of fitness is required to even begin a serious training program; otherwise injuries plus mental and physical fatigue will seriously hamper achieving your goals. Basic fitness in this case means your current interfaces with customers should be mobile-friendly.

Start with your website. If you search for "Google mobile friendly test," you will be presented with a simple analysis tool that will test whether or not your current website is recognized by search engines as being easy for customers to use with a mobile device. Clearly your site needs to pass this test. Beyond that you should also be critical of the presentation of your brand value online in the mobile interface.

- Does the basic information come across in an easy-to-consume manner?
- Can the customer easily contact you by phone or email with a simple click? (They should not have to remember the number or email address to complete this task, just click.)
- If they need to come to your office for some reason, will your address information launch a maps app for navigation?
- Do the video case studies play on the device without the hassle of a separate app or, God forbid, a download?

If you are not comfortable about passing this basic fitness evaluation, and you are also not comfortable with your current digital vendor, find one or two that will give you a second and third opinion. They should happily do this for free for an opportunity to become your supplier.

Next make certain someone searching for you online, whether mobile or not, easily finds your company, but be especially critical of how the search results are displayed on a mobile device. They should be identical, but there are unseen variations that need to be in place for the best mobile presentation. In any case, anyone searching directly for your name should get lots of options for connecting with you online via their mobile device. Test it. If you aren't happy with the result, either hold your current vendor accountable or ask for a second and third opinion. Chapter 8 in my first book, *The Digital Wrap*, is a great place to start in understanding the basics for a service contractor website. If you are truly working your digital wrap, the customer searching for you online via their mobile platform should get loads of information about your company right in front of their nose.

Finally, assess the mobile fitness of all of your other routine communications with your customers. This begins with a commitment to have both email and mobile contact information for all your important customer contacts. I have never once answered a call at my office landline. If someone leaves a message, it comes to my mobile phone and I decide whether or not I want to call them back by pushing a button. Any of my customers or important partners who really need me have my mobile number and my email. You should be able to reach your customers the same way.

Make collecting email addresses and mobile contact information a routine part of your customer intake process. If you are sending them any sort of email or text correspondence that requires them to download and print a document, find a way to change that pattern to a "just click here" routine that presents the information in a way that allows them to take action right away without the hassle of a download. ServiceTrade's Quote Link and Service Link features are great examples of engaging the customer in a manner that invites them to appreciate your work and take action to award you more work without leaving the mobile interface. Send yourself test samples of several of the important correspondences you regularly exchange with customers. Evaluate whether or not you get the value from these messages without putting down your phone. If you are not happy, rework and reformat until you are.

Marathon Training

Once you achieve basic fitness, you are probably already in the top 10 to 20 percent in your market regarding ability to compete. Now it's time to begin the specific marathon training in earnest. Again, this is not a quick tune-up; it's a commitment to building up the muscle and stamina to be competitive in a marathon race. Don't expect it to happen overnight, but instead develop a training plan that will get you there over a period of one to two years. Here are a couple of stories to put your training into perspective:

When ServiceTrade was just starting out, we spent about five months and about $80,000 on our first mobile app design iteration. It never went to a single customer or prospect because we threw it away and started over. We had picked the wrong combination of technologies, and the result really sucked. It worked (sort of), but it was not up to our expectations for our brand, so we literally threw it in the trash heap. We did, however, learn a lot about what we really wanted, and that was a valuable experience. We began the effort anew with a different set of partners who were true experts in the mobile space.

Even large companies need a long training period to get ready for a mobile marathon. About 18 months prior to Chick-fil-A having a mobile app, I noticed that many of the locations began sending cashiers into the drive-through line with iPads to take orders. I'm willing to bet that this was a deliberate marathon training activity to understand exactly how to achieve effective mobile order-taking. Chick-fil-A got more than a year of feedback from "friendly" users to help them get it right for the major launch of the Chick-fil-A One app to the masses.

For the best results, undertake similar training. A small subset of your best customers, or perhaps your salespeople and customer service staff acting on behalf of customers (like the Chick-fil-A cashiers in the drive-through line), are great partners for getting a truly scalable customer mobile experience to the market. Start with a few simple things like having a basic customer service portal on your website where an existing customer can request service and browse a limited set of service history. Make yourself into a customer contact and see what your customers see by spending some significant time browsing with your mobile device and using the interface just as a customer would. Be critical. Remember, this is marathon training and not the middle of a race that you are already losing. There is no point in desperation or exasperation. Take deep breaths and carry on with the training. Expand your muscle and fitness and move ahead to make the adjustments that move toward a competitive marathon outcome.

Race Day

To win the mobile marathon, you need a branded mobile app for your customers just like Starbucks and Chick-fil-A. In addition to the obvious capabilities that are simply carryovers from your website service portal (service history, equipment assets, contract details, quotes, etc.), here are the attributes of the mobile app you will use to pound the pavement competitively over the course of your mobile marathon:

Available in the app store or by scanning an equipment tag: Everyone looks for the apps they need at the app stores hosted by Apple and Google. Your app should be no different. This will mean some work to post it there, but if you have already done the training (that is, the testing discussed above), it should not be a problem. The app should also be available on demand by scanning a tag on a piece of equipment that is covered by your premium maintenance plan. This is the modern day version of leaving a "Call for Service" sticker on equipment. In this case, it is "Scan for Service."

Asset and location awareness: The app should be *context-aware.* Just like the Chick-fil-A app lets me choose the location nearest me for placing my order, your app should default to (be "aware" of) the nearby location or nearby equipment for reference as the most likely candidate for review or service. After quickly navigating to the record of the nearby equipment, the customer can then annotate the record to facilitate better service (such as access-code updates for your benefit, an update from a related vendor that changes your service scope, etc.) or submit a request for service or support with perfect contextual awareness for your staff to respond quickly and accurately.

Self-service: Any information or feature that might help the customer help themselves without contacting you is a good idea. The app should show official service manuals, recent equipment inspection or certification results, original commissioning documentation, likely faults and quick relief guidance (such as how to clear a false alarm), and "Things you should know about this equipment" videos. Self-service is not a loss of revenue for you. Instead it is a powerful customer loyalty magnet, and you should engage it whenever possible to stick the customer more tightly to your premium program.

Real-time collaboration with multimedia engagement: This feature works like placing a FaceTime call. If the customer can initiate a callback to your experts that includes both context (which piece of equipment they are standing near) and video capability, it should be easy to walk them through a relief mechanism for a malfunction. Self-service is better, but quick relief from a malfunction is very powerful as well. Quick relief is easier if you and your customer are collaborating with the same information – that is, the equipment records and your what-you-see-is-what-I-see capability.

Push notifications: Your app should ping your customer when you are delivering value for them. Push notifications are better than email because they simply give a quick heads-up to the user in real time without requiring a pause to check email. Your system will follow up with an email that provides more detail, but push notifications are standard operating procedure for mobile apps. The customer can always turn the notifications off if you are delivering so much value that it becomes a distraction.

Recommended for you: This is the list of repairs, retrofits, and upgrades you have scoped for this particular customer to review and accept. When a customer is in a mood to spend money on something, it needs to be easy for them to spend that money with you. Maybe it is the end of the year and the capital budget is still full of money. Maybe they are having a great quarter and want to plow some of the revenue back into improvements. Whatever the reason, always have a set of recommendations out there for consideration when your customer accesses the mobile app.

The most successful service brands have a mobile app as a defining feature of their premium program. If you want to win, a mobile app is your future. I was very deliberate with the marathon metaphor so that you would envision a long-term plan with multiple plateaus of achievement leading up to race day. If you don't commit soon to the fitness plan, however, it is unlikely that you will be racing with the best competitors in your market a few years from now. When race day comes in a few years, you do not want to be an out-of-shape, flatfooted bystander watching the racers while you hand out refreshments. Start getting in shape now. Work your way toward maximum fitness. Mobile marathon training will begin shortly, and race day is going to be a ton of fun.

THE SIGNIFICANT OBJECTS PROJECT

Rock stars get paid like rock stars because their music makes us feel good. Stories that carry us on an adventure in which a hero triumphs over trouble occupy untold hours of our days via books, movies, television, and theater. We have been programmed since the dawn of time to be moved by images, stories, rhythm, and rhyme. A service experience that takes your customers on an adventure in which your company overcomes trouble so that nothing ever happens with their critical equipment justifies a premium price. Your brand will become associated with feel-good experiences, and the low-price competition that offers only weak sales platitudes and a lower invoice will become irrelevant in your market.

Big brands like Coca-Cola, Budweiser, Burger King, McDonalds, and others historically used music and catchy lyrics to imprint their brands on our psyches. You can probably still sing the ingredients of a Big Mac (two all-beef patties, special sauce, lettuce, cheese, pickles, onions on a sesame seed bun – just did it, no looking). Big-company advertising also used imagery and stories to communicate brand value. You probably remember iconic commercials like the Mean Joe Green Coca-Cola commercial in which Joe gives his jersey to the kid who gave him a Coke and made him smile. "Have a Coke and a smile." These big companies historically spent literally billions to reinforce pleasurable feelings about their brands through images and stories so customers would be willing to pay a premium for their otherwise undifferentiated products. All these advertising habits are changing now as experiences that engage the customer become the new brand-building formula.

Today's dominant brands are being created through such experiences, with most focusing on a mobile technology experience. If you can create an online mobile experience for your customer, they will literally be carrying your brand in their hand everywhere they go. Domino's is one of the first big brands to demonstrate this lesson, and they now command a hefty premium with investors as evidenced by a stock-price-to-revenue multiple that is more than double that of competitor Papa John's. Domino's may not be charging a lot more than Papa John's for their pizza, but they are capturing many more new customers and keeping their buying interest through their online and mobile purchase experience – the Pizza Tracker app. Investors are paying a premium because they are confident in Domino's growth and staying power among a typically fickle pizza consumer segment.

Your digital wrap is your scalable answer to an online and mobile experience that makes customers feel good about your brand. Even if nothing bad ever happens to critical customer equipment, you can earn a premium because the customer experiences all of the great service your company delivers through an online interface. Your technicians become the storytellers who deliver imagery that lights up customers' brains as they see the trouble your company helped them avoid. When your wrap is online, your brand is always at their fingertips. Your company and services are easy to remember, review, refer to, and recall. You can confidently invest in sales programs to add new customers because your digital wrap will keep them engaged and happily paying a premium over many, many years.

Here are the money-for-nothing lessons we hope you remember. We have tried to convey them with rhythm, rhyme, and stories so that they will stick in your memory!

Money for nothing is the feel-good premium. Customers who have good feelings about your company will pay you more money for less work. When they see your great work through your digital wrap, it makes them feel good. The digital wrap is a constant reminder of your brand promise.

Tell a story to sell a service. Stories light up our brains with pleasurable feelings. We are particularly drawn to stories of trouble and triumph. Give the customer a shot of pleasure by showing them the trouble they avoided because your company executed on your subscription program.

Tellin' ain't sellin'! All customers are from Missouri, the "Show-Me" state. So show them your program as part of the sales cycle. A demonstration of how your company uses information for their benefit will close a premium contract much easier than empty sales platitudes promising hard work, caring more, or being family-oriented.

Think like a bank bandit! Slick Willie Sutton robbed banks 'cause that's where the money was stored. Stop sticking up the neighborhood lemonade stand and focus your technology investments on better sales, marketing, and customer service capability. There is 100 to 1,000 times your revenue available in the market you serve, so go take more of it!

How many? How much? How long? Measure your business the way an investor would measure it. Gross margin is important, but the ability to attract new customers, consistently capture more of their business, raise prices, and hold on to them forever is the real measure of the value of your business.

Growing is better than grinding. Growth is valuable to investors, and it is valuable to your prospective employee base. Attracting new talent to your business is a lot easier if you have a vision for growing the company and being more important to your customers and your community. Younger-generation workers want to know they are making an impact on their world. They want to see a brighter future. You can accomplish these things and attract fresh perspectives to your business with a solid plan plus credible evidence of growth. You will also get paid more money when it's time to pass the business to a new owner.

Start training for the mobile marathon. A modern digital wrap strategy means that your brand will go mobile so it's always in the customer's hand. A great mobile strategy means customers are carrying your value with them wherever they go. You are just a tap and a click away anytime they need reassurance that your premium program is working for them.

We are going wrap up *Money for Nothing* with one last piece of scientific evidence that telling a good story helps you charge a premium for your services. In 2009 Joshua Glenn and Rob Walker, a writer and a journalist, respectively, set out to prove that stories can increase the value of everyday objects. While it is tempting to view the goal of the exercise as justifying the value of a writing class by two writers, the results of the experiment are unequivocal. Humans value stories, and they become invested in the objects that reinforce the stories they enjoy.

Joshua and Rob purchased 100 pieces of stuff from garage sales, thrift stores, and related trinket outlets for a grand total of $129. With an average price of $1.29 each, these objects were clearly just worthless trinkets. They then enlisted professional writers to conjure stories related to each piece of stuff to accompany the auction of said stuff on eBay. They were careful to demonstrate that the stories were not actual experiences of the objects, but the stories were clearly entertaining and added meaning to the ordinary trinket. (You can have a look at the items and the details of the experiment by searching online for "significant objects Joshua Glenn.")

The auction value of the storied stuff as measured by sales price on eBay was $3,612 – a return of 2,700 percent. Put another way, they achieved 96 percent gross margin on their sale. Pretty good margin, huh? Clearly a good story helps increase the value of a sale.

So what is the return on your services? How much are you able to charge above what it costs you to deliver? How much more can you charge than your low-price competition who is simply competing on the size of the invoice? Your services are more significant, and therefore more valuable, when you deliver the story describing what happened. The story is what you saw, what you did, why you did it, and what likely trouble the customer avoided because of you. It is the photo and video essay of images that reinforces the value of your brand. It is the online experience that is available to them each time they want to review and learn from your valuable service program.

Humans learn from images, story, rhythm, and rhyme. It has been programmed into us since the days of the cavemen and community fires. Since you are not going to insist that your technicians become poets or rappers, you should at least insist that they relay their good work to the customer in the form of images and stories. When you teach the customer something about their equipment, it reinforces the good decision they made in contracting with you. Over time, the accumulated review of your work will imprint your brand in a manner that is not easily supplanted by the One-Truck-Chuck competitor who is always willing to go lower on the invoice. You will be able to raise prices because your services have become significant through the power of story.

Are you ready to become the rock star of your market? Do you think you can sell a story that shows the customer how valuable your services are? I promise you that building a digital wrap and earning money for nothing is more fun than grinding it out with Chuck over the prices on an invoice. Selling services that make customers feel good about your brand is a very rewarding way to spend a career. Go ahead, be a rock star.

ABOUT THE AUTHORS

Billy Marshall is a founder and the CEO at ServiceTrade, and he is the author of *The Digital Wrap: Get Out of the Truck and Go Online to Own Your Customers*. He is an innovator in the area of technology and subscription sales and a sought-after speaker on topics relating to digital marketing and sales methodology for commercial service contractors. With professional experiences ranging from General Electric to IBM to Red Hat, and as an entrepreneur for technology ventures like ServiceTrade, Billy brings a broad perspective to best practices in customer service, marketing, and sales. Billy graduated with highest honors in aerospace engineering at Georgia Tech and holds two graduate degrees from MIT. He lives in Chapel Hill, North Carolina, with his wife and three daughters.

Shawn Mims runs marketing and product management at ServiceTrade where he is the company's longest serving employee. With a mechanical engineering degree from North Carolina State University, Shawn applies a scientific approach to a chaotic subject: the customer experience. He works to bring successful strategies from consumer and high-tech customer service, sales, and marketing into the realm of commercial service contracting. On weekends you'll find Shawn cooking tasty meals, rock climbing, and enjoying other outdoor activities with his wife and two dogs.

Made in the USA
Columbia, SC
21 September 2020